A Bar Manager's Guide To Controlling Costs

How To Eliminate Theft and Waste To Maximize Profits
by
Thomas Morrell

This book is dedicated to Neal. Thanks for everything! You are a new inspiration.

Table Of Contents

Chapter 1
Understanding Costs

The Goal Of Management

In a work like this, it is important that we define the goal of management in a bar or restaurant. Here it is in a nutshell. **The goal of management is to find the perfect harmony between cost control and customer satisfaction.** You can have both and they are not mutually exclusive, although it can be a challenge to achieve them both simultaneously.

What do I mean by this? Well, simply put, you could give everything away in your bar instead of charging for it. This would make your customer very happy, but would completely ruin your cost ratios.

On the other hand, you could cheat your customer and pour cocktails without alcohol and have a perfect liquor cost ratio. This of course, would ruin your customer service.

As I said, you must strike a balance and always work to maintain that balance. Use your judgment and make decisions. That is what managers do. If it is going to cost you a customer, or you have to comp a drink, it is always a good idea (in my opinion) to comp the drink and ensure that the customer will return.

A Quick Definition Of Cost Ratios

In the restaurant and bar industry, there is a standard method of measuring costs through a simple cost ratio. This cost ratio is always:

$$\frac{\text{Cost Of Products}}{\text{Revenue From Products}} = \text{Cost Ratio}$$

For example, assume that you spend $10 on a bottle of liquor and then sell all of the shots in the bottle for $50 in revenue. In this situation you cost equation would be:

$$\frac{\$10 \text{ (Cost Of Product)}}{\$50 \text{ (Sales From Product)}} = .20 \text{ or } 20\%$$

Just what does this mean? Well, what this means is that for every $5 of sales, you, as the bar owner or manager, must invest $1 in product. Another way of looking at this is that for every $1 that you invest, you can expect to profit $4. In terms of profit, this is a 400% gross profit margin.

Throughout the rest of this book, this is the equation that will be referred to whenever costs and cost ratios are discussed.

Now, obviously, the lower your costs, the more money you make, and that is why you are reading this book. You want to keep your costs as low as possible and make as much money as you can. Inside this book, you will find many ideas and methods for keeping these numbers as low as possible and diagnosing and fixing high costs through waste and theft prevention.

Why Are Cost Ratios Important?

Cost ratios are important as a means to measure the health of your business or the business you manage. Once you set minimum cost ratios (this will be explained shortly) and are constantly measuring your performance against that minimum cost ratio, you can see how you are doing. Are you hitting the minimum? Are your cost ratios high when compared to reasonable goals? Are your cost ratios moving closer towards your goal or farther from it? If they are you are improving efficiency. If you are moving farther away, you are becoming less efficient.

Cost ratios are also important to track the gross profitability of products. Liquor, beer and wine can be very profitable. For example, it is not uncommon to have cost ratios of 20% or less. Again, this means a gross profit of 400% or more. However, this is a gross profit which means profit before all others costs such as labor, dish washing chemicals, maintenance, electricity, rent and other utilities are paid. These can be very expensive costs. (Together these are known as indirect expenses). This 400% profit margin can be quickly reduced by these other costs. Whatever is left over is the net (after all expenses are paid) profit of the bar. As business people, we want this net profit to be as big as it can be. The only two ways of doing this is by lowering our cost ratios, or by lowering our indirect expenses. In many cases we have little control over indirect expenses such as rent and electricity. As such, this book will focus on what we can control. That is our cost ratios.

As though it were not enough to say that lowering cost ratios is a direct way to increase the net profit of a bar, remember that net profit is what produces raises, new stores, bonuses, profit sharing and expansion in a business. Even if you are not the owner and are only a manager, increasing the net profit by lowering your cost ratios can be a huge bonus to your pocketbook! Never forget this.

Minimum Cost Ratios

It is important that you realize that there is a limit to how low you can push your costs. In this book, I will refer to these as minimum cost ratios. If you buy a bottle of alcohol for $10 and do not waste any shots or have any shots stolen from you, you can sell the alcohol in this bottle for $50. This means that you have a minimum cost ratio of 20% (remember $10/$50 = .20 or 20%).

However, in the restaurant and bar industry, mistakes happen, bartenders are inefficient and wasteful, and employees steal. All of these actions will increase your cost ratio above the minimum 20%.

For example, suppose a bartender has a bad pour technique. When they pour a shot, instead of pouring exactly 1.25 ounces, they pour 1.5 ounces. This means that they are wasting .25 ounces of liquor each time they make a drink. This is 15% more liquor than they should be pouring. This also means that less revenue will be taken in from the sale of the bottle.

If 15% of the bottle is wasted because of this bartender's bad technique, you will only take in $42.50 for the bottle instead of $50. This means your cost ratio becomes:

$$\frac{\$10}{\$42.50} = .235 \text{ or } 23.5\%$$

Helping you to push your actual cost ratio as close as possible to the minimum cost ratio is what this book is all about. This means eliminating waste and preventing theft.

Cost Ratios & The Effect Of Prices

The minimum cost ratio is a ratio of your cost to produce a product and the price that you charge a customer for it. You must understand this relationship.

In most cases, you will not have any control over what you pay for product. The price for a bottle of liquor is set by market prices or state regulators, for example.

Prices are another matter altogether. You can, in theory, raise prices whenever you want to. This will lower your cost ratios every time. For example, say you introduce a 10%, across the board price increase. Using our familiar example, you will now take in $55 in revenue for a bottle of liquor that cost $10.

The math on this change works out to be:

$$\frac{\$10 \text{ (Cost of Liquor)}}{\$55 \text{ (Revenue from Liquor)}} = .181 \text{ or } 18.1\%$$

As you can see, raising the price, increases revenues, this lowers the cost ratio. Instead of a cost ratio of 20%, we now have one of 18.1%.

Of course, if you lower prices, the opposite is true. You will increase the cost ratio. For example, if you cut prices by 10%, the above example would turn into this:

$$\frac{\$10 \text{ (Cost of Liquor)}}{\$45 \text{ (Revenue from Liquor)}} = .222 \text{ or } 22.2\%$$

With your cost ratio increased to 22.2%. Sometimes, like with the introduction of a happy hour a bar is forced to lower prices and increase cost ratios.

Of course, raising prices can be a tricky and prices are subject to economic pressures. Sometimes you cannot raise prices and remain competitive. However, sometimes price is no object either. Destination bars, sports arenas, resorts and casinos can often charge whatever they want and people will pay it. You as the manager will always need to carefully weigh any decision regarding pricing and the effect it will have on the bottom line of your bar.

Setting Reasonable Cost Ratio Goals

It is important that you set realistic, but aggressive cost ratio goals. This is _very_ important. You need to understand that there is always going to be some waste in any bar situation. It is inevitable. However, it needs to be your goal and is the purpose of this book to help you reduce waste (and even theft) to the very lowest possible level. Setting impossible goals will only have the effect of causing failure and frustration and in a worse case scenario, staff apathy over costs. This can be cancerous to the morale and profitability of a bar staff.

Cost Control Is About The Aggregate

In the restaurant and bar industry, there is no silver bullet that will make all of your costs magically fall into line. Effective cost control is all about managing and controlling every little point where money can be lost to prevent waste and theft. In essence, cost control is all about the aggregate (that is the total sum) of every little effort that you, your management team, and your employees put forth.

For example, yes it is only a few cents difference in cost between three olives on a martini versus four. However, those few cents count, and if you and your management team eliminate and prevent little problems like that, through effective management, over the course of a month, quarter or business year, those little improvements can add up to tens of thousands of dollars in additional profit for your business. Additionally, every time you see and eliminate a waste or theft, or correct a behavior, you are adding to the efficiency of your establishment and are making your job easier. Efficiency adds up just like savings do.

If you are the owner of a bar, the aggregate of all this effort can be a huge increase in the return on your investment. If you work for a company and mange a restaurant or bar, this, again, can mean bonuses, raises and increases in benefits which everyone always appreciates.

So, whenever you are working, always think about the aggregate. Every little bit counts and is worth attention. Drill it into your assistant managers (if you have any) and your staff members. Remember, it is in their interests too. Profitable restaurants and bars don't go out of business and force former employees to look elsewhere for work and businesses that are not profitable do not offer profit sharing, less costly insurance and 401(k) matches.

If you can create a staff culture that appreciates cost control through the aggregate of efforts, your bar is well on its way to running as efficiently and profitably as it can.

Liquor Profitability

It is no secret that selling liquor in a retail setting can be immensely profitable. This is why so many people want to invest in bars. Let's take a look at a few of the numbers to make sure that everything is crystal clear.

In the United States most liquor bottles are sold in quantities of 750 ml. Converting this to ounces, which is how shots are measured, there are 25.36 fluid ounces in every 750 ml liquor bottle. A standard shot is 1.25 ounces, which means there about 20 shots (20.288 to be exact) per bottle of liquor.

If you buy a bottle of inexpensive liquor at a cost of $8.00 per bottle (which is actually a high estimate) and sell it for $3.00 a shot, you will turn an $8.00 investment into $60.00! This is a 650% gross profit, that does not take into account all those indirect costs of running a bar such as rent, employee costs, etc., but you get the idea that there is a lot of money to be made from liquor.

The last example was using a bottle of well liquor. What happens if the liquor is premium liquor? Well, assume that the bottle of alcohol costs $50.00 for your bar and the shots sell for $8.00 each. Well, now that you know that a bottle contains 20 shots, you know that it will sell for $160. This means a profit of $110 a bottle or 220%. Now, the profit margin on premium liquors is lower, but in reality, you make a lot more money in terms of dollars and cents.

From a bar owners point of view, however, you want to sell as much well liquor as you can. It is inexpensive and has a great return investment. Additionally, you do not have to tie up your capital in expensive bottles that sit on the shelves for years before they are emptied. A well bottle never last to long in a bar.

Consider A Semi-Premium Well

A semi-premium well can be a great selling point for liquor in your bar. A semi-premium well is a well that features lower cost, recognizable name brand alcohols. These are not top shelf per se, but are not bottom of the barrel either.

There is a good deal of financial sense in this sort of a strategy. The most obvious advantage is that you can charge a little more for a semi-premium well. Many people will happily pay $4 for a name brand shot, instead of $2 for unknown well liquor. This can also dramatically help your profit margin. Here is how. Instead of going for the bargain basement vodkas that cost $6 a bottle, you splurge and get a recognizable brand for $12.00 a bottle. A shot of the $6.00 vodka costs $.30. A shot of the semi-premium liquor that cost $12.00 per bottle will cost $.60. However, instead of gaining $2 in revenue per shot sold, you now gain $4. For the added investment of $.30, you are effectively doubling your well liquor revenue.

Customers will often show preference for your bar based on a semi-premium well. They can feel that they receive a better quality in your bar than in others. It is entirely possible that your bar will be better off financially serving a bargain basement well, but you should at least consider a semi-premium well. Ultimately it is your bar and you know your customers best, and are in the best position to make decisions of this kind.

Wine Profitability

Wine, conveniently enough, is also sold in 750ml bottles. This means that we know that, like liquor bottles, there are 20.288 ounces of wine in every standard bottle. Wine is generally poured in 5 ounce portions. This means that for every bottle there are:

$$\frac{20.288 \text{ Ounces Of Wine}}{5 \text{ Ounces}} = 4.05 \text{ Glasses Per Bottle}$$

Wine prices vary considerably across the spectrum from a few dollars all the way to many thousands of dollars per bottle. However, it is not uncommon to sell a glass of wine in a bar for the same price as a wholesale bottle. It is a good idea to get as close to this ratio as possible. In this situation, you would be making a 300% profit margin. However, this is not possible with every bottle of wine. In some cases, you may need to sell two glasses to pay for the bottle, but you should never exceed this amount. This means that the lowest profit margin an owner should expect is 100%.

Beer Profitability

Beer is less profitable than liquor, but it is still a very profitable item to sell in your bar. Additionally, beer is more commonly sold in many bars due to the lower rate of alcohol consumption (a beer is drunk more slowly) and the lower cost of a beer as opposed to many cocktails. Additionally, there is a social element that often makes a beer at lunch, much more acceptable than a martini at lunch.

To get a good understanding of just how profitable selling beer is, let's look at an example.

Assume that you buy a keg of beer for $100. This is a fair price for many of the brand name beers that are sold around the world. In the United States, a standard keg holds 15.5 gallons of beer. One gallon of beer is 128 fluid ounces. A common serving of beer (again in the United States) is 16 ounces. This means that one keg of beer holds:

$$\frac{15.5 \text{ Gallons X } 128 \text{ Ounces}}{16 \text{ Ounces}} = \frac{1984 \text{ Ounces}}{16 \text{ Ounces}} = 124 \text{ 16 Ounce Servings}$$

Now that we know how many beers are in a keg, we can easily calculate the cost your bar must pay to serve a beer. To do this we divide the price of the keg, by the number of beers in it or:

$$\frac{\text{Price Of Keg}}{\text{Number Of Beers In Keg}} = \text{Cost Per Pint}$$

In our example, this works out to:

$$\frac{\$100 \text{ (Price Of Keg)}}{124 \text{ (Pints In Keg)}} = \$.81 \text{ Price Of Pint}$$

You can clearly see from the cost, that selling a pint of beer for even $3.00 can be very profitable. To be exact, this is a 270% profit margin. The above process can be repeated to calculate the cost ratio for any keg of beer.

Now, this example analyzed the cost of a pint of beer from a mass produced brand name beer. These days there are many craft breweries that exist that offer smaller batched beers with all types of style variations. The pricing for these beers will vary quite a bit. As a trend, they do tend to be more expensive. This is largely due to the lack of economies of scale offered by the larger breweries. Although these beers do tend to be more expensive, customers are willing to pay more for them and you can often charge a higher price. Usually, the profit margins will work out to be similar.

Cost Is Never About Cutting Quality

As an effective manager, it is important that you understand that while trying to control costs, it is always a bad idea to do so by cutting the quality of the products in your bar.

If you have an established client base, they have become used to certain standards in your bar. The fact that they keep coming back is testament to the fact that you are doing something right. Customer satisfaction is an invaluable, although intangible, business asset that needs to be protected.

Yes, you can cut the cost of a cocktail by using concentrated orange juice instead of fresh squeezed. However, there is often a marked flavor difference that will be noticed by regular customers. If your prices have remained the same, they may feel squeezed, and if upset enough may not come back.

The same can be said for the alcohols that you pour. There are very inexpensive wines that you can serve by the glass and call a house red or white. However, quality in wine can be very apparent and will again, be noticed by regular guests.

If you can find a product of equal quality, at a lower cost, this can be a great business decision. These can be found, if they are looked for. Talk to different distributors and suppliers and know what they offer. Distributors will be happy to allow you to try their products in the hopes of winning your business. Go to tastings at local wine clubs, and try different whiskeys when you are out. Just remember, as a manager, you always need to be protective of the products you offer. Do not allow their quality to a casualty of your efforts to reduce and control costs. In the long run, your customers will suffer and so may your bar.

Cost Is Never About Cheating Your Customers

A lot of bartenders and bar owners have been tempted to improve their cost ratios and their bars profitability, by cheating their customers. Usually, this takes the form of pouring short drinks (pouring a half shot when a full shot is called for), or pouring a well drink, when a premium liquor has been ordered. Another despicable technique is to fill premium bottles with well liquor.

These practices are reproachable, and should never be used to keep costs in line or increase profitability. The consequences can be disastrous. If customers become aware of this practice, they will stop coming to your bar, tell everyone they know and your business may fail. If, on the other hand, the liquor companies become aware of these practices, they can sue you for trademark damage and take everything you have. Beyond that, this is simply stealing from your customers, who ultimately pay your bills. Always remember to respect your customers. They are the ones who pay your bills.

Good management and effective cost control techniques are more than enough to keep costs in line and make sure that your bar is quite profitable.

Staff Cost Ratio Education

In my personal opinion, it is never a bad idea to make your staff aware of the concept of a cost ratio, as well as the latest monthly cost ratio for your bar. This can be done through memo postings, monthly staff meetings or even just through conversations. Now, most companies do not want to advertise what they make in terms of profit. This kind of information in the wrong hands can cause problems. Avoid dollar amounts, and stick to broad cost ratios ideas like high or low, efficient and wasteful. These numbers and concepts are useful and can be understood without need of the money values behind them.

Informing your staff about cost ratios has many benefits that you would be foolish to ignore. Firstly, it lets your staff know that you are paying attention to, and tracking costs. This helps to put people on notice that any malfeasance such as theft or waste will be caught quickly and dealt with. Nobody wants to lose their job.

Telling your employees about your current cost ratios creates a metric whereby you can measure your employees' performance, and they can measure themselves. In most cases, people want to do a good job. Letting your bartenders know where they stand in terms of cost ratios, is a great way to help them improve and give them a sense of pride. You can also inform them, while at the same time setting a goal. OK, this month we were at 18%, next month, let's shoot for 17.5%. This kind of a challenge can be very appealing. Depending on the ownership and management of your bar, you can even tie this type of a goal into a bonus structure. Depending on the size and volume of your bar, a .5% drop in liquor costs can add tens of thousands of dollars to the bottom line over the course of a year. Paying out $100 per bartender could be a small worthwhile incentive. Another idea is to add money to a bar party fund. This rewards everyone's hard work, and a company party can be a great way to build team spirit as well.

Lastly, introducing your employees to the concept of a cost ratio, and getting them used to using them and setting goals around them, can be a great way to prepare employees for future management opportunities. It is a well trained staff indeed that is completely familiar with the concept of cost ratios and goals.

Flexibility & Experimentation

As I stated before, there is no magic bullet to give your bar perfect cost ratios. Every bar is different and only you can decide what is the best way to control your costs. You need to be flexible and assume an experimenting attitude. Try one method, and if it helps continue. If not, move on or change the method to suit your particular situation.

Also, your employees can be a great source of information and ideas. Do not be afraid to talk with them either. Many bars are loaded with veteran employees from the industry. They will have worked in bars and environments that you may not have. In many cases, they have experiences that can be very helpful. I can tell you for a fact that many of the best ideas that I have encountered in my years in the industry have come from employees working under me.

Always Be On The Lookout For Sales and Discounts

In 1933 the United States congress repealed prohibition. At that point, the federal government passed the responsibility of regulating alcohol sales to the states. From then on, each state has passed laws controlling how bars purchase the alcohol that they will sell retail.

In some states, you can buy alcohol directly through liquor distributors. In some states, government bodies were set up to exercise a state monopoly on the sale of hard alcohol. On the extreme end, South Carolina even mandated that alcohol sold in bars could only be poured from 50ml mini bottles. This law was recently repealed, but stood for many years.

However you buy your alcohol, prices fluctuate over time. Even the state monopolies will have a sale from time to time to control their inventories. It is always a good idea to stock up on inventory when the price is reduced. This means that the costs of producing drinks is lowered and the profit margin is raised. This is always good for a bar's bottom line.

Also, if you operate a bar in a state with privately held liquor distributors, make sure you shop around and always find the best price. This too, will lower your costs and increase your profit margin.

The Easiest Way To Control Costs, Is To Increase Sales

Before finishing this chapter, I want to make one point perfectly clear. In any bar, the most effective way to control and even lower your costs is to increase your sales.

Remember that a cost ratio is arranged like this:

$$\frac{\text{Cost Of Products}}{\text{Sales Of Products}} = \text{Cost Ratio}$$

Assume for the most part, that your bartenders are doing everything that they should. They are using measuring devices and pouring their drinks perfectly. Great. However, one night, a person orders a rum and cola. Instead of making a rum and cola the bartenders accidentally makes a tequila and cola. No one is going to pay money for this. So, they have to dump it out. This kind of thing happens all the time. They have to waste a shot and no revenue is taken in for it.

Assume that the wasted shot cost $1. They do pour a rum and cola and take in $5 of revenue for it. The cost of the rum is also $1. In this situation, so far, the cost ratio looks like this:

$$\frac{\$2 \ (\text{costs for both shots})}{\$5 \ (\text{revenue received})} = .40 \text{ or } 40\%$$

Now, the same person returns later and buys another rum and cola, again for $5. Everything is poured perfectly, and nothing is wasted. Again, the rum and cola costs $1 to produce. Now the cost ratio looks like this:

$$\frac{\$3 \ (\text{costs of three shots})}{\$10 \ (\text{revenue received})} = .30 \text{ or } 30\%$$

As you can see, simply selling one more cocktail has lowered the cost ratio from 40% to 30%. This is a 25% reduction. Now, this is a simple example, but you can easily expand this idea, and see how selling an additional $1000 a month, can really help to minimize the impact of waste. In that case, the cost ratio would be:

$$\frac{\$201 \ (\text{cost of 200 shots plus one wasted})}{\$1000 \ (\text{200 drinks worth of revenue})} = .201 \text{ or } 20.1\%$$

Since, in this example, shots cost $1 and are sold for $5, the absolute minimum cost ratio is 20%. After selling 200 drinks with a waste of one, we find that the *actual* cost ratio is 20.1% which is extremely good. This is why adding to your sales is so important in terms of controlling costs.

Now this concept only applies to waste, theft is a different matter. Someone stealing from you can easily destroy your cost ratios and ruin the profitability of your bar. This subject is addressed in Chapter 3.

Setting Prices

In order to maintain good cost ratios, you need to make sure that you understand how to set the prices in your bar. It is also important that you understand the affect that prices have on your cost ratios.

The first step in setting a price is determining the cost of producing a drink. This is pretty easy. The technique that is shown here, will work for anything. You can use it to figure out the cost of beer, wine, liquor, etc. Just remember it is always:

$$\frac{\text{serving portion}}{\text{package size}} = X$$

$$X \times \text{cost of package} = \text{cost of serving}$$

Let's start with an example to illustrate how this is done. In this example we want to figure out the cost of a Lemondrop. A Lemondrop is made from 1.5 ounces of vodka .75 ounces of triple sec, 2 ounces of lemon juice and 2 sugar cubes. Now, a 750 ml (remember, 750 ml is equal to 20.288 ounces) bottle of vodka costs $7, a 750 ml bottle of triple sec costs $6, a half gallon of lemon juice costs $3, and a box of sugar cubes costs $3.

To figure out the cost of the cocktail, you figure out the cost of each component in the recipe.

$$\frac{1.5 \text{ ounces of vodka}}{20.288 \text{ ounces per bottle}} = .074$$

$$.074 \times \$7 \text{ per bottle} = \$.52$$

This means that the 1.5 ounces of vodka in the cocktail recipe cost $.52. Repeating this process for the triple sec we have:

$$\frac{.75 \text{ ounces of triple sec}}{20.288 \text{ ounces per bottle}} = .037$$

$$.037 \text{ x \$6 per bottle} = \$.22$$

The .75 ounces of triple sec in the cocktail costs $.22. Now, to determine the cost of the lemon juice, you need to know that one half gallon contains 64 ounces. The math is pretty much the same:

$$\frac{2 \text{ ounces of lemon juice}}{64 \text{ ounces per jug}} = .031$$

$$.031 \text{ x \$3 per bottle} = \$.09$$

This means that the lemon juice in a lemon drop costs your bar $.09. Lastly, we have the sugar cubes. Now, let's assume those come in a box of 200. Again, the math is pretty much the same:

$$\frac{2 \text{ sugar cubes}}{200 \text{ sugar cubes per box}} = .01$$

$$.01 \text{ x \$3 per bottle} = \$.03$$

The sugar cubes cost $.03. To finish, we add up all the costs ($.52 for vodka, $.22 for triple sec, $.09 for lemon juice and $.03 for sugar) and come up with a total of $.86. This is the cost of producing one Lemondrop (now this does not take into account labor, dishwashing, etc.). This is the number you need to set the price.

Assume that your bar has a target cost ratio for hard alcohol of 20%. This means that you want the cost of the cocktail to be 1/5 the price, or conversely, you want the price of the cocktail to be five times its cost. Using our example Lemondrop with a cost of $.86, you would need to set the price of the cocktail to $4.30 (5 x $.86).

Now, this is a weird number, and you could probably push it up to $4.50 without any problems. However, doing this changes the cost ratio. Let's look at how.

Effects Of Pricing On Cost Ratios

Continuing with the example of the Lemondrop from the last section, assume that you set the price to $4.50 instead of $4.30. $.86 is exactly 20% of $4.30. However, with the price set at $4.50, the cost ratio changes to this:

$$\frac{\$.86 \text{ (cost of lemondrop)}}{\$4.50 \text{ (price of lemondrop)}} = .191 \text{ or } 19.1\%$$

The cost ratio of producing a Lemondrop has actually been lowered below 20%. This means that every time you sell a Lemondrop, the net effect is to help lower your hard alcohol cost ratio below your target goal of 20%.

Now, let's look at the other side of the coin. If, on the other hand, you thought that $4.50 was to high and instead chose to lower the price of a Lemondrop to $4. What would be the effect on its cost ratio? What would be the effect on your overall hard alcohol cost ratio?

You have to look at the math again. It looks like this:

$$\frac{\$.86 \text{ (cost of lemondrop)}}{\$4.00 \text{ (price of lemondrop)}} = .215 \text{ or } 21.5\%$$

Changing the price, again, alters the cost ratio. In this case, it pushes it above the overall hard alcohol goal of 20% to 21.5%. Now, the net effect when you sell a Lemondrop in your bar is that it will push your overall cost ratio higher, above your goal.

This was a pretty basic example of how pricing can affect overall cost ratios. It is a good idea to review your prices on at least a quarterly basis. At this point, you can compare recipes to their current costs of production. Are they realistic? Do prices need to be raised? Prices fluctuate over time and a review of prices needs to be part of your overall bar management plan.

Increasing Your Sales

There are many different ways to increase your sales. Below are just a few quick ideas that are simple and relatively inexpensive to implement.

Discount Doubles

Discounting doubles can help move liquor. With this idea, you sell a double drink, cheaper than two singles. This might convince someone to buy a double for say $5 instead of just a single for $3. Mathematically this can be a good deal for your bar. Your bar may be receiving a lower profit margin, but in the end, it is putting more money in the bank. This, after all is the end goal of any theft or waste prevention effort.

Of course, you will need to make sure that this practice is acceptable with your local liquor control and will need to observe all laws concerning stopping service to an intoxicated person.

Add A Food Menu

Add a simple food menu that will increase sales (if not already required by law). Peanuts, pretzels, and chips can be added instantly and are available in individual packaging. These can be sold to guests and will not require any kitchen investment, or licensing. Sandwiches require almost no kitchen investment at all beyond refrigeration, and can be added quickly. You can enhance this type of a menu easily with sandwich grills and microwaves that do not require special duct work.

Frozen foods keep very well and along with a deep fryer, can add hot, tasty, inexpensive fried food to your bar menu. These items are always a great seller in a bar. You will need to check with local building codes and fire laws to see if you need to install a hood fan exhaust system. Additionally, you will need to check with your local health department for licensing.

Adding And Promoting Liquors & Mixers

Adding liquors and mixers to your bar can also add sales. Many cocktails now involve energy drinks and customers are more than happy to shell out extra money for these mixers. Also, you should know what types of alcohols are popular at the moment. Make sure you have these and promote them on any menus you have. Liquor companies have partnered with celebrities to make their products part of popular culture. This can help you sell their liquors.

Additionally, you can promote liquors you already have with displays from liquor distributors, branded chilling machines and with shot girl events in your bar. This is something you can organize yourself, although many liquor distributors will be happy to help you with these events and displays that sell and promote their products.

Sales Contests

Sales contests can be a great way to get your staff to sell more of a particular product such as beer, wine or liquor. Essentially, you create a competition between your servers to see who can sell the most and the winner gets a prize.

You can tailor sales contests any way that you need to for your business. You can do category contests (beer, wine or liquor). You can have a contest to see who can sell the most of a particular brand. You can do contest nightly, or over long periods of time. I know managers who have even organized the staff into teams and had a month long contest. This created a bit team rivalry that helped to add to sales and enthusiasm.

As far as prizes, cash is always good, but drinks and gift cards work well too.

Happy Hours

These days, it may seem that people are looking for bargains and ways to stretch their money. The truth is that people have always loved a bargain. That is just what a happy hour is designed to appeal to.

A happy hour, just so we are on the same page is a period during which a restaurant or bar offers discounted food, special low priced appetizers, and discounted drinks. The best time to offer a happy hour is outside of your normal busy hours. This way, your normal busy hours remain so, and you add business and sales during your slower times. This, in theory, produces a net gain in revenue. Happy hours also have the added effect of introducing people to your bar. This means that you may also add customers and sales during your normal busy periods as well

Now, you need to be careful when adding a happy hour. The first thing that you need to do before proceeding is to check with you local liquor commission. Sometimes, these organizations have regulations with discounting alcohol. Make sure you are clear here before proceeding.

Once that is done you need to make sure you construct a happy hour menu that is less profitable, but still profitable. You want to make sure people are getting a deal, but you can't give away the store. Also, start slowly with happy hour pricing. You can always discount more if you need to, but will irritate customers and burn goodwill if you pull back from a happy hour or raise prices.

The last and most important decision you need to make concerning introducing a happy hour is to make sure that the hours are useful to your bar. A happy hour should bring people in when they are not normally there. If you already have busy hours with good sales, leave those alone.

Encourage Tasting

It used to be true that beer and wine options in bars were vary limited. However, in the last 30 years there has been an explosion of craft breweries and wineries. Craft distilling is also beginning to take root in many parts of the United States. These operations produce many very fine, often local, products that you or your customers may not know about.

Talking to your distributor or going to tastings is a great way to expose yourself to new products that may be of interest to your customers. Once you are pouring them in the bar, you can introduce them to your customers by offering tasting sheets. Once customers are more familiar with your products, they are more likely to buy them. Additionally, portioning and pricing on a tasting sheet is frequently the same as several drinks. For example, the wine on a tasting sheet is often equal to several glasses and costs more than a single glass as well. This means you are increasing your revenue and lowering your cost ratios.

Tasting sheets like this one are a great way to introduce your customers to your products.

Beer & Wines Of The Day

Running daily specials on beers, wines and cocktails is a great way to give your customers the feeling that they are receiving a deal. At the same time, you can use this technique to help introduce your customers to new products.

A great time to use this technique is when you introduce a new beer or wine. Maybe you got a good deal on a case or keg from a distributor. If you offer it as a daily special, you will have a better chance of debuting it to your regular guests who may like it enough that it becomes a regular. Often, distributors will offer you special discounts on new products so you can do exactly this and still make a good profit.

If you do choose to run a daily special of some kind, it is not a bad idea to make it known to your guests. If no one knows about it, you will never sell any. You can have your employees tell guests about it, you can print daily special menus, or even get a dry erase board and write it on there for everyone to see. Once your guests become accustomed to the idea of a daily special, they will begin to ask and check out the board.

Special Sheets

One of the most powerful tools to increase sales and influence the decisions of customers is the special sheet. All this is, is a printed menu that features cocktails, food items, appetizers, etc. These items can be available in your bar anytime, but with their addition to the special sheet, they stand out and get noticed.

For example, say you got a really good deal on some premium scotch and want your customers to know about it. Put it on the special sheet. Another good use of the special sheet would be to use it to feature seasonally appropriate cocktails. Say that they warm weather is coming up, showcase all of the summer coolers that your bar can put together. The same is true in winter. People will be looking for warm drinks. Just put a list on your special sheet and watch what sells.

The special sheet also helps with your costs by potentially increasing your sales revenue as well. For example, imagine a customer walking into your bar. It is hot and they want a cooling cocktail. Well, they are thinking about a well gin and tonic. This costs $4. Well they sit down and look at your special sheet. They happen to notice a really tasty sounding special that you have that feature tropical juices and rum. This costs $8. They decide to splurge and go for the $8 cocktail. Well, you have just doubled your revenue. You can say, well they may have just bought two gin and tonics, but the truth is, you never know. Remember one in the hand is worth two in the bush.

To help this scenario play out, give some thought to what you put on your special sheet. They should be items that are slightly more expensive that items you sell frequently. This helps increase the possibility of more revenue. Additionally, feature new and fresh items on your special sheet as a way to introduce customers to new products. You will not be sorry that you did.

Liquor Lists

If a customer is standing in front of your bar, they can look over all of the liquors that you have displayed. However, you may have some that are stored in an area that the customer cannot see or may not notice. What happens if the customer is sitting at the table? How are they supposed to learn about all the products that you offer? Well, you can hope that your servers and cocktailers know all the liquors that you carry, but this is unrealistic. I would be surprised if the manager knew all of the liquors, let alone the server.

The most efficient and easiest way to tackle this problem, and to make sure that your customers can access the information if they want it, is to provide a liquor list on all of your tables.

This list could be paired with the much more familiar "wine list" in a nice decorative book. This way, the customers can refer to it when they want to, and your servers and cocktailers can be trained to point it out to the guests. All of this has the net effect of raising your customer's awareness of your products. That is never bad for business.

Conclusion

In this chapter, we discussed the basic idea of a cost ratio. Working with and achieving a positive cost ratio is one of the most important and difficult jobs a restaurant or bar manager has. Additionally, we discussed several ways to increase sales and lower costs. Now that you have a good understanding of these concepts, as well as the profitability of the products you will be selling, we are ready to move on to discussions of eliminating waste and theft in your bar.

Chapter 2
Controlling Waste

Waste, for the purpose of this book is defined as the unintentional loss of product through negligence, bad procedures, or accident. Waste, along with theft form the two major problems that cause cost ratios to rise uncontrollably and profits to drop.

Remember, that you will never completely eliminate waste, you can only control it. Accidents will happen. Bottles will be broken and bartenders will mix the wrong drinks. As a manager, your goals should be to understand why and how waste occurs, implement procedures to prevent and control waste and to properly train your staff. These steps will reduce waste to a low, controllable level.

The Concept of Lost Revenue

Before we move to deeply into the analysis of waste, I want to make one concept very clear. This is the concept of lost revenue. Lost revenue is the negative consequence of waste. Essentially what this means is that instead of selling product your bar has paid for, you are giving it away and taking in no money. This is lost revenue.

An example, as always, will help to make this point very clear. Imagine that a bartender pours a shot of whiskey. This bartender does not measure the whiskey, but instead pours it out until he decides enough is in the glass. In reality, instead of the 1.25 ounces that should be in the glass, there is 1.75 ounces, or 40% more than there should be. The bartender then sells the shot for $5.

Now, as far as the bar pricing is concerned, 1.75 ounces of whiskey should actually be sold for $7, not $5. In this example, .5 ounces have just been given away. This is all that matters. The wasted liquor is not on the shelf that should be and could be sold to a customer later on for $2. This is the lost revenue, and the damage of waste.

The Flip Side Of The Coin: Overspending

The other side of the coin, where waste is concerned is overspending on your inventory.

Using the example from above, I will illustrate how this can become a large drain on your business' cash flow as well. Imagine that the .5 ounces of liquor that is being wasted costs $.40 cents per shot, or $.20.

Now, imagine that the bartender makes this mistake 20 times a day. Well that means that he is giving away $4 worth of liquor (at cost) each day, or $1460 a year. This is $1460 worth of liquor that you purchased, and did not need to. Imagine if you have five bartenders on staff, and they are all doing this!

Bad Technique

The number one waste of product is going to be bad pouring techniques. Beer, wine and liquors all have special ways that they should be poured. In the pages that follow, I will detail the proper pouring technique for each type of alcohol. This is with the idea that you will have been trained, and can pass the proper techniques on to your staff.

These pouring techniques are taken directly from my other book, *Bartending Basics: A Complete Beginner's Guide* (ISBN 978-1448644681). This book is available from many online retailers.

Proper Pouring Techniques

Instructions For Pouring A Beer

The first step when pouring a beer from a carbon dioxide tap is to bring the glass within a few inches to the tap at a sharp angle like that shown in the picture at right. **Do not allow the tap to touch the glass.** This can break the glass or contaminate it.

Open the tap all the way by pulling it towards you. The beer will pour out. The close proximity and the angle of the glass shorten the fall of the beer and greatly reduce the amount foam that will result.

As the beer fills the glass, gradually reduce the angle of the glass so that eventually the beer is pouring straight into the glass like that shown in the picture to the right.

This has the effect of creating foam as the pour finishes. This is called "coaxing a head". This move will help ensure that the beer has a proper head and the full flavor of the beer can be enjoyed by the guest.

DO NOT simply open a tap and allow the beer to foam into an unangled glass. This will cause the beer to foam and fill the entire glass with beer.

If you pour too much head, do not simply displace it by allowing the tap to run and fill the glass to the appropriate level like the picture. This is very wasteful.

Instead, scoop out the excess head with a spoon and repeat the pouring process with a partially filled glass. If needed, scoop out any excess head a second time.

Liquor Pouring Techniques

Jigger pouring is the pouring of alcohol using a jigger. A jigger is a small metal measuring tool that will all but eliminate waste, if used correctly. The jigger will have two cups in most cases. One will be a full shot and the other will be a half shot. Which one you use will depend on the recipe for the cocktail you are making.

To use a jigger, hold it over the glass. This way, if you spill any liquor it will fall into the glass. This is shown in the picture below. Fill the jigger all the way and when the measuring cup is full, stop pouring. Then tip the measuring cup so all of the liquor falls into the glass. Do not fill the jigger up and tip it while liquor continues to pour into the glass. This is called a "tail" and is wasted liquor and lost profits.

A jigger is a great tool to ensure that only the right amount of liquor is poured into a cocktail. This tool eliminates waste.

Pouring with a jigger takes a little practice. You will spill a little at first. To help with this, get a bottle, a jigger and a pour spout. Fill the bottle with water and just start pouring. A little practice this way will help you a lot in the long run.

The other means of shot measurement is called a "free pour count". Free pouring is the process of pouring the liquor right from the bottle into the glass or mixing tin. There is no measuring device in this process. Instead, the bartender counts, in their head, while they are pouring the liquor. Generally, a "four count" is used for a shot and a "two count" for a half shot. Count quickly. There is no need to say "Mississippi" or "Hippopotamus" while you are counting. Simply count off "one, two, three, four" and stop.

When using a jigger fill it all the way over the glass. Quickly dump the liquor into the glass when it is full. This will help prevent spilling.

You will not pour exactly one shot on a four count when you are beginning to free pour. You will need to develop and refine your sense of timing. This is also done with practice. Start free pouring and use your count. Pour off one shot, and then with a jigger, measure what you have poured. If it is too much, count faster. If there is too little liquor, count slower. After a little practice you will get the hang of things.

Jiggers Are Tools Of Consistency

A good way to look at a jigger, and to sell it to your customers, is as a tool of consistency. When a bartender measures the alcohols and other ingredients into a cocktail, it will be the same cocktail each and every time that they step into your bar. This means that if your recipes are good, the drinks will be good every time and your customers will begin to expect this. When your customers can count on good drinks in your bar every time they walk in, much of your hard work to control costs and run a profitable bar will be done. Some people will always complain. This is something you need to accept and learn to manage.

Tails

When a bartender fills a jigger and dumps it in the glass, but continues to pour liquor from the bottle, it is called a tail. Tails can be a cancer to liquor cost ratios and is a terrible waste of your product. It is not an exaggeration to say that when a bartender pours a tail, they are wasting between .25 and .50 shots **EACH** time. For a $4 cocktail, this represents $1-$2 in lost revenue for each cocktail they make. On a busy night, this can quickly run into the hundreds, if not thousands of dollars. If you think your bartenders are pouring tails, you must find them and put an end to it quickly.

Most of the time, a bartender who pours tails does not even realize they are doing it. Somehow, when they learned to bartend, they picked up a bad habit and it has stuck with them ever since. Bad habits can be hard to break. In situations like this, training is the best answer. If you see one of your bartenders pouring a tail, stop them, point it out, and demonstrate the proper procedure. This way, you know that they have been trained properly. Once this has been done, you can discipline them as you see fit (again in accordance with your human resources department guidelines or your attorney) up to replacing them in your bar. However, the first line of defense should always be identification of the problem and training where tails are concerned. You may have a good bartender and employee who simply needs to refine their technique a little. In most cases, one time will be enough, but you will need to remain vigilant to make sure the habit does not return.

Tails that are not accidental or part of bad habit are theft and are covered in the next chapter.

Pouring Wine

As I mentioned in Chapter 1, a standard wine pour is 5 fluid ounces. However, it is not customary to either fill up the glass that the wine is poured in, or to measure the wine as it is being poured. This means that your servers and bartenders will need to be able to pour a glass of wine by sight alone. Your employees will need to become accustomed to doing this. This can be hard and it is the manager's challenge to properly train the staff.

In my experience, you need to set your bartender's up for success. In most cases, people want to do a good job and follow the rules. You can help control waste simply by providing bartenders with the proper tools to do their jobs.

A wine gauge is just such a tool. A wine gauge is one of your bar's wine glasses that is filled with a durable substance to the level that you want your wines to be poured. By durable substance, I mean something that is not going to spoil such as rice, barley, or coffee beans.

Five ounces look different in different glasses. Help your bartenders by making a wine gauge like these. These glasses are filled with five ounces of rice.

With this tool on the bar, your bartenders can quickly check the levels of the pour visually. This helps to accustom them to what a proper pour should like in the glass. Additionally, you as the manager can quickly check their work by comparing any glasses of wine waiting to go to tables against the gauge.

This is a very simple (not to mention cheap) two part system to help control your wine pours, and by extension costs. The first is providing useful, easy to use tools for the bartenders to do their jobs correctly. The second is showing them that you will be checking their pour levels to provide useful constructive feedback.

Custom Drink Guides

Every bar should have a customized cocktail guide. This guide should be specific to your bar and is designed to be used by your bartenders to see exactly how management wants them to pour each and every drink that you offer.

This guide should list:

- Drink Name

- Drink Recipe. Be specific and list **EXACTLY** how each cocktail should be mixed.

- Proper Glass

- Proper Garnish

- Retail Cost

If you work in a bar that does not have a drink you have a problem. If your bar does not have a guide, bartenders will not know how to mix a drink and will just guess, often wastefully or wrong. If, on the other hand, your bar is using a commercially published guide, you need to make sure that your cocktails are priced for the recipes in that book, not something else. If the prices do not match the recipes, you could be losing a lot of money.

If you do not have a drink guide, or are not sure if prices are pegged to the one you are currently using, making a "correct and official" guide with the above information should be a top priority. This will take some time, but it is a good investment in protecting your cost ratios.

Also, once you have completed your bar's custom drink guide, make sure you store the electronic format somewhere safe. It will save you large amounts of time if you choose to update or change recipes later on down the road.

Proper Garnishing

Along with making sure that every drink has a recipe in the bar, you need to make sure that every drink has a standard garnish. Garnishes are important. They make drinks look attractive and add perceived value. They also make drinks more fun. Eating the garnish on a Bloody Mary is often just as pleasing to the palate as the drink itself.

Garnishes are needed to make drink attractive and add value. However, you want to make sure to control those costs.

However, all of those olives, asparagus, cherries, celery and pineapples are not free. To bring them into your bar and put them on the rims of your drinks, you need to pay money for them. You want to make sure they are used appropriately, but not wasted. If a bartender is putting seven olives in every martini, they are wasting these olives (olives for example can be pretty pricey).

In your custom drink guide, you need to have information about the standard garnish that goes with any drink and in what quantity. You want your bartenders to know these just as much as the drink recipes. They should never be guessing or using their own creative flair.

Head Control

In *Bartending Basics: A Complete Beginner's Guide*, I made the point that the head on a beer is essential to the flavor of the beer. However, from a manager's standpoint, there is another problem with a beer that has no head on it.

It may not seem like a lot of beer, but filling a glass all the way to the rim with beer adds one or two ounces of liquid beer to the finished product that should not be in there.

This is a waste of beer, and consequently, results in lost revenues to your bar.

Let's look at how wasteful this is. Assume that your bartender fills each of glass to the rim. Let's assume that this is two ounces of extra beer for each pint. Let's also assume that you sell one keg or 124 pints a week. This means that you are wasting:

2 ounces X 124 pints sold X 52 weeks per year = 12,896 wasted ounces

$$\frac{12,896 \text{ ounces}}{16 \text{ ounces (one pint)}} = 806 \text{ wasted pints per year}$$

Assuming that you sell one pint of this beer for only $3, you are literally losing $2418 per year just from improper head portioning. This number and the fact that your customers are receiving a flat, flavorless beer (I have known many customers who would send a beer without a proper head back) should ensure that you always make sure the beers from your bar have a proper head on them.

The glass on the left has more beer in it than the one on the right. Without a proper head, the beer lacks flavor and is overfilled and wasteful.

Using The Right Glass

It does not matter if you serve a shot in a wine glass, pint glass or shot glass. If the shot is properly measured, the same amount of liquor is in each glass. However, when you make drinks with expensive mixers like fresh orange juice, energy drinks and Bloody Mary mix, using the wrong glass can waste mixers, and money.

Mixing a vodka and energy drink in a 16 ounce pint glass as opposed to a 12 ounce highball glass requires the addition of several extra ounces of mixer. Just like the last section, those little ounces add up and throw your cost ratios out of line. Energy drinks easily cost your bar $2 per can. This can mean costs to your bar of up to $.20 per ounce of wasted product.

In your custom drink guide, make sure you specify which glass is to be used with each cocktail and make sure that your bartenders know these. Ask questions. If you see a drink go out in the wrong glass, make sure you call attention to it and correct your bartenders.

Three Ball Pour Spouts

Three ball spouts are a relatively recent addition of the equipment that you can buy for your bar. These spouts have three metal balls inside the spout that precisely measure out the amount of alcohol that is dispensed. Each time the bottle is tipped upside down, only a certain amount will come out.

This system offers you the appearance of free pouring, which customers love to see, with the efficient measurement of spirits, which is great for business. Most customers will not realize that shots are being measured unless they look very carefully while the drink is being poured. Most won't.

Three ball pour spouts automate shot measuring while giving the appearance of free pouring to your customers. These are both great helps to controlling costs and creating a profitable bar.

These spouts are available in many color and capacities. You can order for one quarter ounce all the way to several ounces. Additionally, these spouts are also sold calibrated for the metric system as well and range from 5 mL all the way to 100+ mL.

These spouts can help to control your costs significantly. If they are attached to every bottle, there is no jigger to forget and no wiggle room with the free pour count. These spouts are more expensive than other types of pour spouts (these can cost upwards of $50 per dozen), but they are well worth the price of the investment.

One last thing to consider with three ball spouts is that everything wears out eventually. It is not a bad idea to test your spouts periodically to make sure they are still properly calibrated. A bar full of spouts that are measuring improperly is worse than a bad bartender.

Computerized Pouring Systems

I want to include a few quick words on computerized pouring systems. This is not intended to be a complete discussion on these systems. These systems are rapidly evolving. For more information, or the most current info, consult bar trade magazines. These often contain both advertisements and discussions of the most current systems available.

It is possible to completely eliminate waste in a bar using computerized pouring systems. The downside to this option is that these systems can be fairly expensive. It will be up to you to decide whether this system is appropriate for you bar. To decide whether one of these systems is appropriate for your bar, you will need to do a simple cost benefit analysis. To do so, compare the cost of the system against the average waste in your bar (this will need to be estimated by you) times the number of years the system is expected to be in place.

Along with eliminating waste, theft is all but completely eliminated with one of these systems through one mechanism or another.

Along with eliminating waste and theft, these systems can add a great deal to the efficiency of your establishment. Shots on a gun and mixing stations put all of the ingredients a bartender needs, literally, at the push of a button. This means no fumbling for ingredients in a reach in refrigerator, or looking for a liquor bottle. These systems also allow the use of larger one gallon bottles. This cuts down on the need to change pour spouts and grab inventory. Also, depending on your local liquor laws, this may allow you to capture quantity discounts on the larger bottles. This means your bartenders can spend more time serving drinks and generating revenue than stocking their bar and finding ingredients.

Consistency is another great attraction for these systems. These are the ultimate in pre-portioned drinks that will be the same each and every time. Again, if your recipes are good and priced appropriately, much of your work in controlling the costs in your bar will be done.

Shots On A Gun

One of the most common forms of automatic alcohol dispensing systems is to dispense alcohol directly through a soda gun. With this type of system, there is a button on the gun for each type of alcohol.

When a bartender wishes to make a drink, say a rum and cola, he would press the rum button and then use the soda gun to add the cola. Simple as that!

These systems can be directly interfaced with bar POS systems to automatically ring in any drinks. Along with the fact that liquor is locked up in the back room and bartenders have limited access to it, this almost completely eliminates theft in the bar.

These systems are great for the basic well liquors that will be poured in any bar. Remember that these are the ones that will be stolen the most! For non-well alcohols, some of the other systems that will be described may be more appropriate.

Wireless Computerized Pour Spouts

The latest technology in automatic bar portioning and inventorying is a system of wireless, microchip enabled, automatic pour spouts. These spouts contain an internal mechanism that automatically pours the exact amount of alcohol you determine each time the bottle is turned upside down just like three ball spouts. However, these spouts also communicate wirelessly with a backroom computer that automatically tracks the inventory. These systems can also be set to automatically enter the sale into the POS system as well.

Since these types of spouts are the latest and greatest, they are also the most expensive system available as of the printing of this book. However, this is a very exciting new addition to the bar manager's toolbox for controlling costs. As these systems become more common, the prices should come down.

Wired Backbar Spouts

The wireless technology that is built in to the last system that is described adds cost to the system. For bars that are out of view of the customers (such as service bars), there is a more economical option.

This is the wired pour spout system. This system is exactly the same as the wireless ones described above, however, instead of using wireless technology, a cable connects the pour spout to the tracking computer. Again, through this computer connection, inventory is automatically updated. Additionally, these systems can be connected to a POS system.

Automatic Mixing Stations

Automatic mixing stations are a step beyond shots on a gun. These mixing stations are in effect, automatic bartenders. The bartender is in actuality, just the machine operator.

With these machines, a glass is placed underneath the mixer and the ingredient buttons are pushed. The machine then automatically dispenses customizable pre-portioned amounts into the glass.

These systems can also be interfaced with bar POS systems to automatically ring in the drinks. Additionally, these systems can also be interfaced to generate automatic monthly and spot inventories.

Again, with the alcohol out of the bartenders control, theft is all but eliminated. However, with the mixers now being pre-portioned and control, waste is even more greatly eliminated too.

Preserving Wine

Distilled alcohol and beer in a keg both have long shelf lives. In fact, with a few exceptions such as Irish Cream, distilled alcohol can sit on shelves for quite a long period indeed. Years in fact. That is why cowboys in the Old West always ordered and drank whiskey. It was the only stuff that wouldn't go bad without refrigeration. In fact, this is why distillation became popular in the first place. The process preserved the harvest until it could be consumed.

Unfortunately, the same can not be said of wine. Wine can be a very expensive product depending on the varietal and the vintage. Of course unopened wine can happily sit (of course cared for properly) for years as well. However, if you are pouring wines by the glass from bottles, you have a very short window indeed between when you open the bottle of wine to when it has gone bad and is good only for cooking or pouring down the drain.

The main culprit in this situation is oxygen. When a bottle of wine is sealed with a cork, or ever increasingly synthetic corks or best of all screw caps (yes they actually have the lowest failure rate), the wine is not exposed to oxygen. When the bottle is opened, the oxygen immediately rushes in and begins to spoil the wine through a process known as oxidation. This will ultimately spoil the wine and make it taste like wet cardboard. The name of the game in extending the life of an open bottle of wine is to minimize the contact between oxygen and the wine. There are three methods for doing this that we will discuss.

Wine Seals

Wine seals are absolutely necessary to extend the life of a wine. These little stoppers are inserted into the mouth of a bottle of open wine with the lever in the picture below in the up position. Once the stopper is securely in the bottle, the lever is flipped into the down position (as shown in the picture). This action expands a rubber doughnut inside the bottle. This makes a very strong seal which prevents oxygen from entering the bottle from the outside atmosphere.

Rubber wine seals are absolutely necessary for preserving wine.

Rubber wine seals are a very necessary component for preserving wine, however, they do not remove the oxygen that is in the bottle to extend the life of the wine. They only prevent more oxygen from getting in. To actually remove the oxygen, these seals must be used in conjunction with one of the other methods that will be described..

Gassing Wine

Argon is a type of gas that is present in small amounts in the Earth's atmosphere. In fact, you are breathing it right now as you read this. Argon is a member of the gases known as "noble gases". Helium, used in balloons, is another type of noble gas. These gases are called "noble" because they are chemically inert, meaning they do not react with any other chemical. This means that they do not react with the chemicals in the wine and break them down like oxygen does.

Helium was mentioned as a noble gas that could be used to preserve wine, but because it is lighter than oxygen, ultimately the oxygen will displace the helium and oxidize wine. This is not true with argon. Argon is actually heavier than oxygen and will displace any oxygen when sprayed into an open wine bottle.

However, argon alone is not enough. One company, called Private Preserve, offers a proprietary blend of carbon dioxide, nitrogen and argon to preserve wines. This proprietary mix isolates and keeps oxygen away from the wine. This helps the wine maintain its flavor and dramatically increases the time you can keep a bottle open to serve quality wine to your guests.

Private Preserve™ is a wonderful product that is simple to use and dramatically increases the lifespan of your wine. Photo courtesy of Private Preserve. For more information, visit www.privatepreserve.com .

However, this product is not only good for wines. If your bar has large investments in high end scotches, brandies, cognac and tequilas, this product can also help to prevent oxidation in these products as well. If you own a bar and serve wine or spirits, you should definitely consider using this product.

Wine Vacuums

When an argon gas mix is sprayed into a wine bottle, it displaces the air (which contains oxygen). Another method for removing the oxygen from a bottle of wine to help preserve it is to suck the air out with the aid of a hand operated vacuum pump, like the one show below.

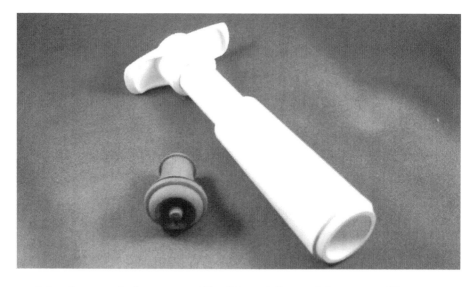

A hand pumped wine vacuum like this and the special stopper will remove much of the oxygen from an open bottle of wine. This will help preserve the wine.

These pumps are inexpensive and easy to operate, but they must be used with special vacuum seal corks. You will need to buy a separate cork for each and every bottle that is to be sealed.

This method will help to preserve the wine, but since a perfect vacuum, containing no oxygen is impossible to create, the wine will not last forever. Also, in my opinion, gassing the wine is more effective. However, these can help to extend the life of wine. You will still need to track how long the bottle is open and, when it is nearing its expiration date, push it as a special.

Dating Wine

It is always good practice in a bar to date any bottle of wine that is opened. Wine only has about three days before the oxidation sets in and begins to seriously degrade the product. This is true even if you are gassing or vacuum sealing the wine.

You do not want your night bartender opening a bottle of wine and not dating it, only to leave it on the bar. Then, five days later, your day bartender, who doesn't know any better, pours a glass of this oxidized wine for one of your guests. The flavor of the wine will be terrible, the guests will assume that you serve poor quality wine (or have bad bartending habits) and will not buy anymore wine. Who knows, they may not even come back to your bar. All of this can be avoided by simply writing the date on each bottle as it is opened. Any wine over three days old should not be served to a guest. It is better to waste the wine than give a bad glass to a customer.

Of course, you do need to make sure you are educating your bartenders about wine oxidation and training them to look at the date on a bottle before serving it. It is also a good idea to train your bartenders to put the date on the back of the bottle in a discreet location. Many wine enthusiasts like to look at a bottle of wine. This is as much a part of the art as the liner notes on a CD. You do not want them looking at the bottle's label only to see a two day old date, written in black permanent marker across the front.

Selling Wine By The Glass vs. Wine By The Bottle

If you have any say over the wines that are offered in your bar, it is a good idea to select them carefully to protect your bottom line.

You need to think carefully about this problem. The more bottles of wine that you have open, the less likely it will be that you sell all of them before some of the wine goes bad. Remember you only have a couple of days. Many small bars with extensive wines by the glass will find that they dump out more wine than they sell.

You should have a red and a white for sure. These will be your basic house wines. A nice cabernet/merlot mix will answer well for the red wines. Cabernet drinkers will love the body and merlot drinkers will find the wine quite pleasant as well. In recent years, pinot noirs have become popular as well due to their appearance in cinema and the excellent pinot noirs coming from California and Oregon. If you pour a second red by the glass, it should be a pinot noir.

White wines by the glass are a little harder. While a nice blend will answer well for many red wine palates, the same is not true for white wines. A riesling is sweet, while a pinot gris has a crisp refreshing acidity that helps to cleanse the palette. These are very different wines and a sweet wine drinker will not be happy with the pinot gris. You should always make sure that you offer a sweet and a dry white wine, but try and limit it to those two if possible.

Champagne is a wine that you need to be careful about offering. Champagne will lose its carbonation even faster than it will go bad rendering it unservable. Also, champagne is an expensive product to be pouring down the drain. Unless you have a strong breakfast rush and serve a lot of mimosas (some bars do) you should probably avoid champagne. One option you can consider if you are determined to carry champagne is a split. A split is a little bottle that serves about two glasses. These can satisfy the champagne drinkers without making them buy a full sized bottle. Instead they buy the whole split. This way, your costs are not in jeopardy from waste.

Also, make sure you bartenders will not open a wine that is only served by the bottle to pour by the glass. Although it is good customer service, it can be terrible to your costs. Remember you want to find the perfect balance between cost control and customer service. If you have a decent selection of wines by the glass, there should be a wine that will make the guest happy. Remember, they can always just buy the bottle if they want it bad enough.

Tracking Dates On Other Spoilable Products

Paying attention to spoilage dates on other products in your bar is an absolute must too. This needs to be done for two reasons. Firstly, you need to do this to make sure that you are protecting the health of your guests by not serving spoiled products. Secondly, you need to track dates to make sure that product is not going bad and being wasted. Examples of products to keep an eye on are juices, fruits, dairy products, egg whites and coffee products.

Product rotation is a mandatory tool to make sure products are not going bad. This is the simple placing of new product behind older product to ensure the newer product is used first. This should definitely be part of your training program!

If product is going bad, you need to reduce the amount of product that you are ordering at a time. Reduce the amount of product you order and keep on stock to ensure that product is not going bad before you can use it.

Working With Vendors

Assume that you want to run a cocktail with fresh berries. Fresh berries can go bad very easily and you are not sure that you will use a full pound in the seven days between your produce deliveries. What do you do to prevent spoilage and waste?

In this situation, the first course of action would be to talk to your produce supplier and tell them about your problem. These businesses survive by selling their goods to your business. They need you and want to make you as a customer just as happy as you want to make your customers happy. In most cases, you can work with vendors and set up multiple delivery days if you need to.

Another option is to discuss will call orders with your suppliers. This is when you go to their location and pick up the product that you need. Any good supplier will be happy to help you. If they argue with you and try to tell you that they cannot supply you on multiple days, or permit will call orders, you should look for another supplier.

Running Daily Specials To Avoid Waste

In Chapter 1, one of the ideas suggested to help increase sales was to run daily specials. There is no reason whatsoever that you cannot also use this technique to prevent waste from occurring.

If you have a bottle of wine that has been opened and is approaching its spoilage date (but hasn't crossed it), it would be a great candidate for a special of the day. If you wait and the wine goes bad, it will be a waste, but if you sell it at half price, you can recoup your costs and maybe still make a profit.

This also works for juices. If you have some orange juice that is going to pass its expiration date, try running a sidecar as a cocktail of the day, or maybe a screwdriver. If you sell enough of these, the product is not wasted.

Giving Away Wine

Another way to dispose of wine that is about to pass its expiration is to give it away. This may seem odd, but it can be a big positive for your bar in the long run.

The biggest appeal for literally giving the wine away is that, instead of being wasted, you are introducing your customers to one of your products. If you give them a taste for free, they may buy a glass then and there. They may buy a glass on their next visit. At the very least, you have educated your customers on your products which should never be looked at as a bad investment.

Additionally, a free tasting like this can buy the goodwill of your customers. Purchasing goodwill is never a bad investment.

Consider Fresh Squeezing

Fresh squeezing juices is all the rage in may bars and restaurants. Customers love the perception that they are getting a fresh and refreshing drink. They also love to stand at the bar and see the drink being made. This makes the process of getting a drink more fun too.

However, there is a business sense to fresh squeezing juices as well. Citrus fruit in the skin, in a refrigerator will last quite a while. In fact, fruits in the skin will last longer than most juices in the refrigerator. As a way to stretch your fruit budget, consider investing in a nice display juicer and squeezing juices to order. Your customers and your bottom line will both be happy.

A fresh fruit juicer can help stretch your fruit budget while adding perceived value to your bar's drinks.

Changing Blown Kegs Properly

When the beer in a keg runs out, the keg is said to have "blown". This means that the keg needs to be changed.

Changing a keg improperly can be a great waste of beer. There is often foam left in the beer lines that will need to be cleared or "bled" out. To do this, the tap is opened and you wait until liquid beer pushes all of the foam out of the line and runs out. You then quickly shut off the tap.

Now, if you have long beer lines (such as from a basement to the third floor) and the beer is pushed with higher pressure gases such as nitrogen, this process can become a little tricky. Liquid beer can mix with the foam and result in the waste of up to a gallon of liquid beer each time you change a keg. Obviously, this is bad for your cost ratios.

The easiest way to prevent the loss of lots of beer is to bleed the lines into a pitcher. This will capture the liquid beer which will settle to the bottom of the pitcher after a minute. Then the beer can be poured for guests.

There are also new, high tech systems that have been developed by brewers that will shut off the flow of beer out of a keg once it detects foam instead of liquid beer. These systems can be a great help and will all but eliminate waste from this kind of operation. There is a cost upfront that you as the owner or manager will need to weigh against the projected loss of beer that these devices will prevent. You will need to decide which is best for you. To install these devices, it is often best to speak with your beer distributor. If they cannot install them for you, they can certainly point to someone who can.

Measured Shot Glasses

Measured shot glasses are another tool to make sure that liquor is measured properly. Of course, this only works when someone orders a shot of something.

Marked shot glasses can be a handy way to ensure a full shot (but not more) is poured each and every time. This glass has been overfilled to make the line more visible.

These glasses have a line printed on them that is the fill line when a specific amount of liquor is poured into them. You will of course need to make sure that fill line is set to the same level you want to be pouring. In most cases, this will be 1.25 ounces, but many bars have different shot pours. Also, if you are reading this outside the United States, your shots will be calibrates in milliliters.

Free Pouring

Free pouring is the pouring of alcohol without the use of any type of measurement tool. Instead of measuring the flow of alcohol out of the bottle, the bartender is supposed to "know" how much is coming out and stop when the appropriate amount has been dispensed. Bartenders will usually count to themselves (in their head) while they are pouring.

Free pouring is a great selling point from the point of view of the customer. Most people feel that they are getting a good deal when they see a bartender free pouring. There is less talk of weak drinks and the absence of the taste of alcohol in a bar that free pours.

The downside to free pouring is that it can lead to a great deal of waste. Without any way to monitor, test and confirm how much alcohol is being dispensed with each shot, your bartenders can be pouring out much more alcohol than has been paid for. This can destroy proper cost ratios and waste thousands of dollars annually. If, you, as a bar owner or manager, want to operate a free pouring environment, you need to make sure to read the next section and implement such a procedure.

Pour Testing

If you, as a bar manger, make the decision to allow your bartenders to free pour, you should make sure that they are taking pour tests. A pour test is when you have your bartenders pour what they believe is a full shot into a graduated cylinder, which measures how much liquid was poured. Of course, you need to make sure they are being tested with water, not alcohol. When the bartender is done pouring the shot, they can see how close they were to the correct amount and adjust their technique as needed.

Many bars make their bartenders complete a pour test each day before they begin their shift. Often, they will need to spend 15 minutes or so practicing, and then do so in the presence of a manger who can then verify they are ready to start pouring alcohol correctly. This gets them in the right mindset and accustoms them to the proper feel of a shot every shift. This is a great way to safeguard your costs in a free pouring bar.

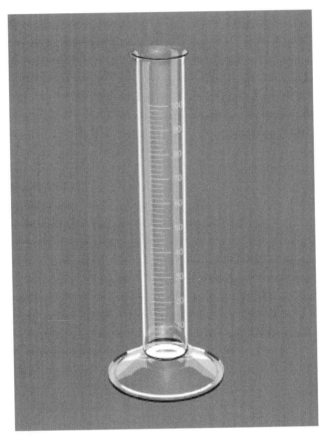

A graduated cylinder is a glass or plastic cylinder with measurements marked on it. This is an essential tool for effective pour testing.

Some bars go even farther than testing their bartenders just before their shift, many will even make their bartenders take a pour test several times during a shift. The idea behind this is to make sure that the bartender does not get lazy and is constantly being made aware of their pouring technique as well as the fact that their pours are being monitored. This is great practice, but make sure you are testing at appropriate time. You, as the manager, can also call for a shot and measure it in the back office.

If you decide to allow free pouring in your bar, you need to have some sort of pour testing to protect your costs and make sure your product is not being given away. The steps described here are a great place to start.

Standardize All Glassware

Without glassware in a bar, you cannot conduct business. However, you should always give thought to the glasses in your bar. Standardization is one of the hallmarks of an efficient organization anywhere in the world. This is no less true concerning the glasses in a bar.

You will of course have many different types of glasses in a bar. For example, there will be beer glasses, wine glasses, shot glasses, chimney glasses, etc. However, you should only have one type of shot glass. You should only have one type of bucket glass. Having many different types of one particular class of glassware only creates confusion. It is very helpful for your bartenders to learn what a proper shot should look like if there is only one glass into which they can pour.

This is not to say that you cannot have multiple wine glasses, say one for red wines and one for cold wines. Just do not have multiple types of red wine glasses. This only leads to confusion, waste and lost profits. Also, if you can no longer order one type of glass (sometimes they do stop making them) it might not be a bad idea to replace all of that type of glass in your bar with a new available line. Yes, this can add costs upfront, but the standardization can save you money in the long run by avoiding waste.

Standardize All Garnishes

Anyone who has ever done the ordering for a bar knows that all those oranges, lime, lemons, grape fruits, pineapples, cherries, olives, onions, asparagus, garlic and celery that garnish the rims of glasses are not inexpensive. In fact, sometimes these items can be very expensive indeed.

For example, consider premium Sicilian bleu cheese stuffed green olives. These little guys can be down right pricey! You as the bar manager or owner need to make sure that your profits are not walking away on the lips of drinks. For example, three olives is a standard garnish for a martini, not six. A Bloody Mary can be garnished with a lemon and a lime, or olives, or celery, or garlic, or pearl onions, or asparagus, or any combination. It is not necessary to have <u>all</u> of them. You should set exactly what is expected and what is standard on every drink and make sure that every drink goes out exactly how you specified it should.

It is entirely possible to make very attractive drinks using garnishes without going overboard and giving away the bar.

The Garnish Tray Is Not A Snack Bar

Employees will often make use of the garnish tray as a snack bar. This may seem like a small point, but, again, all those olives, pineapples, cherries and citrus fruits cost money (do you see a theme yet?). If you are not careful, your employees can eat enough to put a dent in your cost ratios. Always remember to keep an eye on this.

This sort of a situation is not an especially serious one, and the best way to correct it is with a verbal reminder that those are not there for the employees, but the customers. You can also tell your employees to bring a snack if they are hungry. If it becomes excessive, you can always follow your proscribed discipline procedures as needed to make sure this stops.

Keeping Flies Out Of Spirits

Flies can be a huge problem in a bar. They are attracted to the fruits and juices that are used in bars, as well as the sweet caramel coloring that is used to flavor and color many liquors. Nothing is worse to the image of your bar than a customer returning a premium scotch that is full of flies. In addition to the damage to your bar's image, that liquor (and maybe the bottle) will then need to be dumped out. This is a total waste of alcohol, and the money that was used to buy it. Any manager worth his salt will make sure that this sort of a situation is avoided, as it can really damage your cost ratios.

Good housekeeping policies are a must. Make sure chores such as taking out the garbage, mopping, bleaching floor drains, and putting garnishes in the fridge are taken care of every night. Beyond that, you can make sure your bottles are protected by using the right pour spout.

There are pour spouts that are designed with fine plastic meshes over the opening, like the ones shown below. This is small enough to let liquor flow out, but also keep flies out. The only downside to a spout like this is that they do not work especially well with thick liquors like an Irish Cream.

Pour spouts with this plastic meshes are more than enough to eliminate the problems of flies in your liquor.

Tracking Waste

It is a great idea to create a sheet where your managers or bartenders can record drinks that are poured by mistake, spilled, etc. This information can be absolutely priceless in figuring out where your liquor, beer or wine is going.

To fully communicate exactly what happened, you need to make sure that you have a place to record the date, product that was wasted, and who wasted it. Each piece of information helps to communicate the whole story of the incident. From these tidbits, you can figure out if you have a bad bartender who is constantly wasting liquor, or why you are missing a bottle of vodka (one was broken for example).

Date	Product	Amount	Reason	Bartender	Manager
1/2/2010	Whiskey	1 shot	spilled by customer	Neal	Mike
1/7/2010	Rum	1 shot	mixed with tonic	Neal	Mike
2/5/2010	OJ	1 Gallon	past expiration date	Dave	Rob
2/9/2010	Merlot	.5 bottles	over 3 days old	Cynthia	Cathy
2/11/2010	Amber Ale	1 pitcher	from keg bleeding	Jim	Rob
3/4/2010	Whiskey	1 shot	mixed wrong mixer	Neal	Mike
3/7/2010	Scotch	.5 bottle	fruit flies in bottle	Chris	Jim A.
3/17/2010	OJ	1 Gallon	past expiration date	Steve	Walter

An example of a waste sheet. By studying this you can gain valuable insight into the operations of your bar. For example, Neal appears on here several times suggesting more coaching is needed for him. Also, orange juice appears to be spoiling regularly. This suggests overordering.

You can also identify problems in your bar and fix them based on information from a waste sheet like this. For example, say you see that a particular bottle of liquor keeps getting broken in the well month after month. This happens, as some points on bottles are notoriously weak. Each time this happens, for the safety of your guests, you will need to throw out the liquor. Well, based on the pattern that you detected through the waste sheet, you can rearrange your bottles and eliminate this problem.

One of the biggest hurdles you will face when trying to implement a program like this one is getting your employees to use it. Make sure that the sheet is in a convenient, quickly accessible location. Putting it right behind the bar is a great idea. Additionally, you will need to make sure your bartenders and managers are in the right frame of mind. You need this information, so stress to them that product that is missing, that is not on the waste sheet will be considered theft. This will help motivate them and furnish you with the knowledge you need.

Conclusion

As a bar manger, waste will be the easier of the two problems that you encounter. Waste occurs when people are in a hurry, are not trained properly or systems are not in place to prevent product spoilage. All of these complications can be overcome with some thought, care and patience, as well as diligence. Employees can be trained to remain calm and follow specifications. Pour spouts that keep flies out of the eighteen year old scotch can be bought, and contests to sell wine that is nearing its expiration date (again not over) can be held. This all requires good management instructing good people on how to do their jobs properly.

In the next chapter, we will discuss the harder of the two problems a bar manager faces when trying to control their costs. This is the problem of theft. Theft is much harder to fight. With waste, often an employee will not even realize they are doing it until you point it out to them. Then, they will correct their behavior, because most people want to do a good job. With theft, a person knows they are doing it, and know it is wrong. They don't care. Worst of all, they will hide it from you. It will be up to you to prevent it, find it and eliminate it when you do.

Chapter 3
Theft Prevention

Why Do Employees Steal?

The reasons that employees steal can be numerous. People will steal when they need money. Perhaps they are late on rent or a car payment. Perhaps they are going on a vacation and have come up short on spending money.

Often, people will steal out of a sense of entitlement. They feel that the business owes them more than they get. They will not even think of theft as wrong as they are "owed" the money.

Sometimes people will steal out of simple greed. They want more money than they have and they do not care how they go about getting more of it. This type of thinking is wrong.

In reality, there are many more reasons that an employee will steal from the bar that they work in than can be covered in this book. You do not need to understand them. In fact, if you have worked hard and are now the owner or manager of a bar, you are probably wired in a manner that would prevent you from understanding the mindset that would make theft permissible. You probably don't even know how to go about stealing from a bar. However, it is your job to prevent it all the time. That is why this chapter, with explanations of techniques to steal from a bar, was written.

What Employees Steal

By and large the easiest and most commonly stolen items by a server or bartender are "server produced items". What are these? These are items that the server has complete access and control in producing. For example, a dessert is a server produced item if the server can go get the dessert and take it to the table without having to involve anyone else. If, on the other hand, a server has to ring in a dessert to the kitchen and wait for them to make it for him, then it is not a server produced item. Sodas, coffee, desserts, salads and appetizers are all commonly server produced items.

Bar drinks on the other hand are not generally server produced items where the server is concerned. Instead, they have to ring these items into the bar and wait for the bartender to make them. They cannot easily steal these items without being in collusion with the bartender.

However, the same is not true of the bartender. They are put in a position of trust over a highly valuable inventory and can easily steal liquor and money if there are not proper systems in place to prevent it. If you have suspicions of theft, the first question you should ask is "What would they steal?" Your investigation will then have a logical path.

Trust But Verify

It can be very difficult for a manager to think that the people that they work with can be stealing right under their nose. As was stated earlier, if you have risen to a position of trust in a restaurant or bar, your mind is not likely wired in a manner that lends it to thoughts of theft. You probably find it hard to understand. Also, you probably like many of the people that you work with and do not want to believe that they are capable of theft.

Well, the sad truth is that theft in restaurants and bars does happen and can cost lots of money. The fact is theft is quite common in the hospitality industry. Also, if you are a manager in a restaurant or bar, you have also accepted the responsibility of preventing theft and catching the guilty parties when it does occur.

This is not to say you cannot like your employees. This is not to say that you cannot trust them. This is only to say that you need to be constantly verifying that they are doing what they are supposed to prevent a climate that can encourage theft from developing. Ronald Reagan said it best. Trust but verify.

This Is Not Personal. This Is Business

I have worked in the restaurant and bar industry for decades. The relationships that are formed in these high stress, yet high fun environments can be lasting and very rewarding. You often develop a sense of camaraderie with the people that you work with. This, in all honesty, can be a difficult obstacle to overcome when the matter of theft comes up. No one wants to believe that someone that they work with and like is a thief. That is one of the hardest challenges of a bar manager. However, for the financial health of a business, you need to check into any suspicion and make sure you conduct a thorough investigation. Always remember that this sort of thing is just business, it is never and should never be personal. Also remember, in an environment that is as cash driven as a bar can be, nothing can be more toxic to a person's reputation than an accusation of theft. For that reason always be very discreet in your investigation until you are actually certain.

What Do You Do With A Thief?

I am not an employment lawyer or an attorney of any kind. I have no special training in human resource management beyond practical experience. As such, I am not qualified to offer advice on how you, or your company should address an employee that is suspected of theft, or how the laws of your state permit you to proceed. Human resource disputes can result in expensive lawsuits if not handled properly. Business owners and managers operate under heavy burdens and are expected to act accordingly at all times. As such, for the most correct and relevant information to any particular situation, consult a qualified employment attorney. An additional source of information that is no substitute for the advice of a qualified attorney is your state's labor department. They are always happy to inform employers as to their responsibilities under the law.

How Employees Steal

As a restaurant or bar manager, it is very important that you understand how theft occurs in a restaurant. It might seem odd that I am going to go through and explain many different techniques in which an employee may steal. However, without this information, you will be powerless to detect, let alone stop theft in your establishment. This is why, in Las Vegas and casinos all over the world, security staffs employ convicted cheaters to spot and stop future cheating. The FBI has also used similar techniques where check fraud and document forging are concerned.

Types Of Theft

Simple Theft

What I like to call simple theft, is the most basic forms of theft that will occur in any restaurant or bar. This is simply when an employee takes in cash for an item and pockets the money. The item is not rung into the computer, POS, or cash register. The customer is often oblivious to this action happening right in front of them. In all honesty, why should they notice? It is not their problem and they have handed over money to a seemingly trusted member of the staff. As far as they are concerned or will notice, they have paid in full.

Simple theft can also be pretty hard to combat and catch. Since things can often be busy, and this is when this type of theft will often occur, it is easy to lose track of things. Employees can be running around and you and your assistant managers will be pretty hard pressed to monitor each and every money transaction. If you tried you would only drive yourself insane.

The best ways to detect simple theft are to look for the traces that are left behind. Firstly, any bar or restaurant will have a cash register. It might be a simple stand alone cash register, or it might be a POS terminal that is connected to a wider computer network. Either way, these machines will all have the option for a "No Sale". This is a button that is pushed that opens the cash drawer without adding any money to the machines counting. This function is included for situations like making change.

Often, a person involved in simple theft will be manning a cash register/POS terminal. They will be carrying out many transactions involving cash. It would be suspicious to the manager and the customer if they completed the transaction without the cash drawer opening. So, they will often hit "No Sale" to pop the drawer open. This makes everything look normal to a casual observer. However, each time a "No Sale" is hit; cash registers and POS systems make a record of it. How you access this information will depend on your equipment, but it is almost always available. To look and see if someone is involved with simple theft, examining the number of "No Sales" that they have is a great place to start.

If you have determined that someone has a suspiciously high number of "No Sales", another technique to catch simple theft is observation. Simply watch, discreetly if possible and see what you can see. Surveillance cameras can also be a great help in matters such as this. Watch, record if possible, and see what you find. Once you detect simple theft is going on, catching someone doing it is pretty easy.

Beyond catching someone carrying out this kind of activity, there are steps that you can take to make things much harder for this type of theft to exist. The easiest way to prevent simple theft is to make sure all managers have an active presence in the bar. Thieves are cowards by nature and will shrink from the act by the simple fact that a manager is in the bar and not in the back office. Spend 10 minutes of every hour just standing and watching in your bar. This alone will let people know that you are paying attention and guarding your operation.

Another great way to combat simple theft is to make your customers demand a receipt. Of course cash registers and POS systems will not print a receipt without a transaction. They definitely will not print one for a "No Sale". This leaves most thieves unable to offer a receipt when a theft has occurred. If you post signs that say **"YOUR ORDER IS FREE IS YOU DO NOT RECEIVE A RECEIPT"** at every cash register, this will make customers alert you if you do not receive a receipt. They will serve as your watchdogs simply for the hope of a free round of drinks or lunch. A free lunch to catch a thief is a great investment.

Sneaking In Alcohol

Sneaking alcohol into a bar may seem like a weird idea, but this is another very easy, very common way for a bartender to steal. The idea behind this is very simple. If a bartender is selling lots of alcohol and keeping the money from those transactions, a monthly inventory, when compared with the monthly revenue, will show that alcohol is missing that has not been paid for. This can lead to suspicion and the bartender getting fired.

Now consider if the bartender goes to a local liquor store and pays under $10 for a bottle of well vodka. They can almost always buy the same brand that your bar uses. If they sneak this into the bar, pour out of this bottle, and then keep the cash from these transactions, they will be stealing lots of revenue from the bar, but the inventory will not reveal it. Using this method, a thieving bartender can turn a $10 investment into almost $200 (depending on how much they are charging for the shots). This practice is most common with hard alcohol, but I have heard of particularly brazen (or stupid) people sneaking in whole kegs!

If a bartender is doing this, they will most likely sneak in their bottle(s) when they first come on. This creates an opportunity to catch them. The best way to do this is to simply count the number of physical bottles in the bar before the bartender comes on and after the bartender comes on. It is not a bad idea to make sure that everyone knows you are doing this. It will again help to make everyone aware that you are on the lookout. Also, make sure that your count is accurate. You don't want to wrongfully accuse anyone because you miscounted a single bottle.

Watering Down Alcohol

A similar practice to the sneaking in of alcohol is the watering down of alcohol to cover up theft by preserving the inventory's appearance. This can be pretty hard to detect, especially with clear alcohol like vodka, or heavily flavored alcohol like gins. Although, in my experience, not all bartenders are smart and I have even seen this practice tried on whiskey. Of course with colored liquors, this makes it look lighter and can often tip off to the practice. Just because someone steals does not mean they are smart.

The best way to protect against this practice is to make sure your bartenders know to never fill up a bottle with anything. This includes pouring a cheaper liquor into a premium bottle, water into a bottle, or marrying two half bottles of the same alcohol. Other than creating an opportunity to cover up theft, this can also expose your bar to lawsuits from liquor manufacturers out to protect their brand.

Stealing Bottles

It is a bold thief that will steal a whole bottle of alcohol, but this does happen from time to time. Often, the person that is stealing a bottle is doing so for personal consumption and is doing so for one of two reasons. The first of these reasons is the liquor store is closed or they do not have enough money to buy a bottle on their own. The other reason that a whole bottle might be stolen is because the thief is under the legal drinking age and cannot legally purchase their own. As a result, most practitioners of this kind of theft are underage.

There are two very easy ways to combat this problem. First is to do the quick bottle count that will be discussed in more detail later in this chapter. The other is to keep as much of your alcohol locked up as possible.

Reservoir Tickets

Stealing using a reservoir ticket is a modestly complicated process that I will attempt to make quite clear in this section. It should be pointed out that this theft technique is only a concern in locations with a computerized POS system. This method is complicated, but can be very costly. Given enough time and a check that is large enough a server or bartender can steal quite a bit of money.

Everything begins when a server or bartender has a check that was paid in cash. Instead of closing this check out in the computer system as paid to cash, the server or bartender keeps the check open.

Now, when the server begins a new tab, they can split off items from the old tab and add them to the new tab. This of course only works if the two tables order something in common. For example, say the first table that paid in cash had a margarita. The second tab also has a margarita. A margarita is a bartender produced item, so it is an easy item to steal for a bartender. Using this technique, the thief would transfer the margarita from the first check to the second check. This way, when the second table is ready to go, the thief can print up an acceptable itemized bill that will not be in questioned by the guest.

If everything goes as planned, two margaritas have been made, two checks will have been presented, two margaritas paid for but only one margarita will have been rung into the computer. One of the margaritas which was paid for in cash will never be accounted for. Although the bartender took in money, the computer does not know they need to remit it to the house, so they keep the difference. This is the theft.

Customers will never be able to help you detect this kind of theft. From their point of view, everything proceeds just as it should. However, from a managerial standpoint, this technique is fairly easy to detect if you are vigilant.   First and foremost, you need to make sure servers and bartenders do not have any paid checks floating around in the computer system. Checking who has checks open in the computer system and asking why they are open will go a long way to making sure that this type of theft is hard to commit in your bar. It will show that you are paying attention to this aspect of the bartender or servers job.

Additionally, every item that is input into a restaurant POS has a time code attached to it. Most of the time, this is displayed when you look at a check in the system. What you want to look for to spot this type of theft, if you suspect it, is time codes that don't make any sense. For example, a soda rung into the computer at 2:30 pm when the majority of the check was input after 9:00 pm does not make any sense. This would be a prime case for asking questions and investigating further. You may have found a thief, but you have to be looking.

Abusing Voids Or Deletes

A void or delete is the removing of an item from a check inside a computerized point of sale system. In most systems, this action can only be done with the authorization of a supervisor. This authorization is given in the form of entering a code into the computer through the swiping of a magnetic card or the entering of a numerical code.

It is very important that the system for having an item deleted from the computer system is very tight. This system can be easily abused if there are holes in the system and it can cost a bar thousands of dollars.

First and foremost, make sure that the people that have the ability to delete items from the POS are trustworthy. If they are not, you need to make adjustments right there. A person with this power can easily steal hundreds of dollars a night and can cover their tracks pretty well.

Secondly, avoid using numerical codes for managers and supervisors. These can easily become known in a small establishment and can be used without the supervisor's knowledge. This again, can lead to hundreds of dollars in theft each night. This is also very hard to catch unless you suspect it. Instead of using numerical codes, make sure all employees with the power to delete items from the POS use magnetic cards. These are much more secure as the codes are much longer (12 digits) and will not become widely known in the bar for misuse.

You also need to make sure that there is a proper procedure for requesting a cancel or void. Your employees should know that when they make a mistake, it needs to be taken care of there and then. Don't permit them to wait until the end of the night to present you with all of their mistakes from the last eight hours! This creates an opportunity for them to request voids for items that have already been paid for. They may not even realize they are doing it. People can forget. This is exactly what you are trying to prevent!

Also, it may seem like a basic point, but you need to make sure that employees must request a void or cancel from another, authorized employee. Don't just leave a magnetic card that can be used for voids lying around for them to use. This is just a bad procedure that is too tempting for some people.

Remember, that people are not above asking you, as their manager, for a void falsely just to pocket the cash. They may have a straight face even when they are lying to you. Whenever someone asks you for a void, make sure that you are asking questions to show that you are paying attention.

Assistant Managers As Accomplices

Assistant managers are not above being involved in theft. They have the ability to alter checks in the POS and are subject to the same temptations as other people. Hopefully, your vetting process will weed out potential thieves, but you need to be cautious none the less.

The best way to protect yourself from this kind of theft is to personally track their activities inside your computer system. You can look at what items they are voiding, comping, canceling, etc. You can see who they are performing these manager functions for. Compare the amounts they are doing to what is average and reasonable in your bar and make inferences from that. When you are in doubt, ask them to explain anything that you do not understand.

Contractor Theft

Theft is not limited to employees alone. In a bar, you will need the services of many tradesmen. You will need construction workers, janitors, carpet cleaners, linen suppliers, deliverymen, etc. Many of these people will need to be in the bar after hours to complete their jobs. After all, you cannot put in a new tile floor while your customers are trying to get drinks.

This can present many challenges to the bar owner or manager, and many opportunities for theft from unscrupulous contractors.

You need to be on your guard to prevent theft in situations like this. The first line of defense is to supervise contractors as much as you can. A watchful eye is often all that is needed to keep them in line. Vendor theft is a crime of opportunity. If they see a chance or a lazy manager, they may be tempted to act. They will not, however, make a plan to steal your product in most cases. They will simply not be comfortable enough in your bar to do this.

There may be situations where you cannot supervise all of the vendors and contractors that work in your bar. In situations like this, you need to keep as much product, as you can, locked up. Also, if you have security cameras in your bar, make sure they are on, and that the contractors know they are being watched. Even if you don't have a security system, there is nothing that says you cannot bluff and say you do. Fake cameras like we will talk about shortly can help as well. Quick bottle counts before and after when the contractors perform their work is a great idea too. Make sure you have exactly as many bottles when they are done as you did before they started.

Adding Handwritten Charges Tickets

If your bar has a computerized POS system, these computers will print computer generated guest checks for your customers. Although, it is bold, employees can write additional charges on these checks and then present them to your guests. I have personally seen this.

Say for example, a table had a pitcher of beer that was not rung into the computer system. The bartender or server could say something like "Oh, I forgot to put this pitcher on the check", and just write it on there in front of the guest. The guest will then, in most cases, just pay the bill. If they pay in cash, the server can then pocket the difference and never ring the pitcher into the computer.

There are two ways that you can detect and catch this type of theft. The first way, is that you can be alerted to it by your customers. Many people would not think twice about a situation like this. If they had the beer (or whatever), they will just pay the bill and be done. However, if they are suspicious by nature, or have worked in a bar before, they may smell a rat and alert management.

The other way that this type of theft can be detected is by going through the discarded checks and looking for handwriting on computerized guest checks. You would not believe how careless someone who is stealing can be. They will often leave telltale evidence behind for anyone to find. You as a manager should always keep waste paper baskets near your computer terminals. This is good housekeeping. However, it also makes it possible for you to go through the discarded paper looking for evidence of theft. This should be a periodic chore that you perform to help prevent this type of theft.

The best way to deal with this type of theft is prevention. If you have a tight system where servers or cocktailers cannot get products from the bar without having first rung it in to the POS, this type of theft is much harder to achieve.

Team Theft

It has already been explained how employees will steal items that they produce themselves and then sell to customers for cash. However, sometimes, employees will team up and steal together.

Here is an example of how such a situation might evolve. Say a bartender works in a restaurant where few customers come and sit at the bar. Instead, they sit at tables in the bar and prefer to be served by cocktail servers. The bartender cannot sell drinks to customers for cash, and the cocktail server cannot pour their own drinks to sell to customers for cash. The bartender and the server are friends and over drinks one night they come up with a plan. The cocktail server will ask for drinks from the bartender, who will pour them without a ticket, and the cocktailer will write them in by hand on the guest checks and pocket the cash. At the end of the night, they will split the money.

This example details a serious breakdown in the cost controls (i.e. no ticket, no product which we will discuss later) in a bar. The best way to prevent this sort of situation from developing is to enforce the cost control systems and procedures in your bar. Make sure that "No ticket, no product" (to be discussed) is an sacred rule in your bar. Check from time to time. Also be on the look for handwritten tickets. You cannot rule out a situation like this developing, and a team like this can cost a bar a lot of money in just one night.

Friends & Family

The friends and family of employees can be some of the best customers of a bar. They will often come in and hang out while their friend is working and buy drinks while they do.

A problem can occur in a situation like this, however. It is often the case that an employee, who would never think of stealing under normal circumstances, will have no problem giving away free product to friend and family. They may not even think of this as stealing, although it is. Make sure your employees know this.

To help fight this problem, it is always good for a bar manager to know the friends and family of their employees if they come into your bar. After all, it may be the case that they are regulars and a manger should always know these people. It is also a good idea for a manager to keep an ever watchful eye on their employees when friends and family are in the bar. Do regular check audits at times like this to make sure everything is on the up and up.

Additionally, you should also fight this problem through education and policy. Make sure that you have a policy in place that prohibits giving away free product at all times. Also, make sure that your employees know that giving away free product to anyone, including friends and family is a serious breach of discipline and can result in termination.

Stealing For Other Coworkers

Unfortunately one of the most common forms of theft in a bar involves one employee pouring and serving a drink to an off duty employee. The theft simply comes from the fact that this drink is not rung in to the cash register or the POS system. No money is ever exchanged. The drink is just given away. Another form that this type of theft can take is a free liquor upgrade from say a well drink to a premium liquor.

This kind of theft can happen for several reasons. The simplest reason that theft of this kind occurs is out of some sense of doing a favor for a coworker. There can also be the implication that for not charging for a drink, the stealing employee will receive a good tip (although less than the cost of the drink) from the drinking employee.

The best way to prevent this type of theft is to require employees to keep receipts for their drinks (this is for their protection as much as anything) and to perform random check audits on all employee checks.

One thing you want to keep in mind is that you want to make sure your employees are not stealing for coworkers. What you do want to avoid is to scare your employees away from frequenting your bar. Honest employees who come in and pay for their drinks can be a great asset to a bar and should be encouraged. You just want to make sure they pay for what they drink!

Ringing In Lower Priced Items

A bartender that knows they are being watched will often choose to ring in lower priced items, and in turn collect money for higher priced ones. For example, they make a vodka and orange juice using premium vodka that costs $8.00 per shot. However, a well vodka and orange juice which costs $4.00 is entered into the cash register or computer system. The bartender can then pocket the difference when paid in cash. This is a theft of $4.00. This kind of theft, when repeated many times a night, over many nights can wind up costing lots of money. Additionally, unless you are paying attention to the bottle in each bartender's hand, this type of theft can be harder to detect. On the surface, everything looks appropriate.

Where you can detect this type of theft is in the total liquor cost ratio (this can take some time and be costly) or by analyzing the bartender's checks once you have conducted some observation and know which bottles were used. Another possible method to detect this kind of theft is to use a sting of the type that will be discussed later in this chapter.

Stealing For Personal Use Offsite

Everybody likes steak and premium cocktails on a camping trip. Nobody wants to pay for them though. Most people do pay for them, but some people like to "borrow" a few things from work before heading out of town. I have seen it happen more times than I would care to mention. Sometimes, employees who are not even working will come in and take what they need on their way out of town if you are not on your guard.

Always keep an eye on who is in your bar or restaurant and when they are in there. Keep employees who are not working out of employee areas to help protect your inventories. Also, never ignore anyone with a bag! A backpack in the wrong hands, in the wrong place, can cost your business a lot of money.

Giving It Away For Tips – Still Stealing

In my bartending career, I have often been offered a "big tip" for something inappropriate. This can be serving someone without their ID, serving a minor, or serving an intoxicated person. It can also be something much simpler, such as putting more alcohol in a drink. Of course, I have never agreed to such a proposal. However, that is not to say that every bartender will be so resolute.

The good thing about this situation is that this type of theft is a lower occurring type than the others. While someone who is sneaking in a bottle of vodka to pour from is making a conscious effort to steal, the perpetrator of this act is succumbing to a rarer temptation that is offered by a customer. They might not even think of it as stealing. They may just do it so someone will stop hassling them. However, this type of theft can lead to more pernicious types and needs to be stamped out just as much as any other.

This type of theft, and let's be clear it is still theft, can be very hard to detect. Really, the best line of defense for this type of thievery is a watchful eye. Keeping your ears open, and maintaining a presence in the bar also work great. Your presence can also help your bartenders not give into hassling with your support. Over time, this can show up in your liquor costs, but will be hard to detect. Training is also a good way to prevent this. Make sure your employees know that this behavior is still theft and is subject to the same consequences as any other type. Also, a good manager will train their employees on the proper ways to deal with these situations so they are not tempted to take the customer up on their offer.

Drinking On The Job

It is a sad reality of the bar industry that many employees cannot make it through a full shift without a drink of alcohol. Additionally, many of them feel entitled to free alcohol given their profession. This is certainly not the case. No one is ever entitled to anything above their agreed compensation. Anything that is taken other than what has been agreed to is still theft. Additionally, in some states it is illegal for a bartender to drink while on the job and it definitely can present a safety hazard. If your bar is in a state where it is legal for a bartender to drink behind the bar, you simply need to make sure that what they are drinking has been paid for.

This type of theft is fairly easy to fight. First, keep the alcohol that is open and in use in an area that is open to view. It is never a good idea to keep open alcohol bottles in walk-ins, back rooms or the like. Removing the temptation and opportunity to steal, and drink on the job will go a long way to eliminating this problem. Beyond that, check what people are drinking. Smell it. Look inside coffee cups with lids and water bottles.

Don't let people keep drinks behind the bar. This is a bad practice to be in anyway for housekeeping reasons. Drinks get spilled at bad times, drinks get left and spoil and can stink and attract flies. Instead, make bartenders (servers as well), drink and dump. That is, drink what you can, and throw away the rest. I have worked with managers who only allowed employees to drink from conical paper cups. They had no base so they could not be set down. People drank and then threw the cup out. If someone does not have a place to store their stolen alcohol, again they will be less likely to steal it for personal use or to drink on the job. Also, someone, say brining a flask or bottle to work, would also be less likely to pour themselves a drink in a situation like this.

Customer Theft

Although theft by your bar's customers is probably the least common type of theft, it does happen and you need to make sure your bar it protected from it.

These bottles are too close to the bar and can easily be removed by a guest when the bartender is not looking.

First and foremost, always make sure that someone is in the bar area and that customers are never left alone with your products. Don't put it past anyone to just grab a bottle and leave. I have seen this happen more times than you would expect. Make sure your bartender's know that they must stay in the bar area and make sure that it is never left unattended. I have seen even the most seasoned bartender's nonchalantly leave the bar unattended to talk to a friend or use the restroom. Also, don't keep product in an area that is out of sight to the bartender. Doing so is just asking for problems.

Beyond making sure someone is always in the bar to keep an eye on things, make sure your bar is setup to keep as many things out of reach of the guests. If they can't grab it, they can't steal it. This is why most bars keep their liquor on a back wall or on an overhead shelf. Make sure your bar does too. Only keep the most basic well liquors close by for immediate use. The same goes for wine, cigars, and even fruit as well. It does not even have to be valuable for a customer who has been drinking to steal. I have even seen a two week old fish stolen from a display case in the lobby of a restaurant. The fish was not fit to eat, but the customer stole it anyway after having been drinking in the bar. He even paid for his tab, just stole the fish.

Cash Register Balance Checks

When someone is stealing and operating a cash register, they will often simply mingle the money they have stolen with the money that is in their cash register. It would look suspicious if, at the end of every transaction, they simply threw all the money in the tip jar. Eventually someone would notice.

Many POS systems will allow you to run a balance report for a cash register. This report will give you the total amount of money that should be present in a cash register at any given time.

This report can be worth its weight in gold to make sure that your bartenders and other employees are doing exactly what they should be. With this report, you can do periodic audits of the cash register drawer to make sure the money is as it should be.

Running periodic cash register balance checks is an absolute must for any manager in an effort to prevent theft. This should be done at least once a shift. If this type of report is not available on your POS, consult your IT support and make sure that it is made available. Also, it is a good idea to make sure that your staff knows that you are auditing the cash drawers. This will help to make them more nervous and less likely to steal.

No Ticket No Product

One of the easiest ways to control the environment of a bar or restaurant to prevent theft of product is to live and die by the principle of "if it is not rung into the POS, the item is not produced". Make this company and house policy and enforce it relentlessly, as the manager.

This will force your servers and bartenders into the habit of entering any item into the computer before it is made or taken to the table.

This will also make it possible for you as the manager to perform random check audits. You can look at a table, see they have a dessert, and check to make sure that dessert is on their check in the POS system. If it is not, then the server will have some explaining to do.

Tickets On The Bar

A similar approach can be used to help prevent your bartenders from having the opportunity to steal by way of the bar itself. If a customer is sitting at the bar, it is a great idea to require that the bartender keep an updated POS check in a glass in front of the guest. This again will prevent the bartender from being able to present the guest with a drink, quote a price and pocket the cash. Again, make this a policy and religiously enforce it.

If a customer has cashed out, there should be a printed receipt sitting in front of them. So, again, you as the manager can perform random audits and will have visible evidence that items are being rung in to the POS system. Also, again, infractions of this policy suggest mischief and can quickly point out a thief. Treat any violation of this policy as suspected theft and deal with it accordingly.

Bag & To Go Box Checks

Backpacks, bags and to go boxes should always be a cause for suspicion when working in the restaurant or bar industry. These provide easy means to carry out large amounts of product to a person's car. These items should never be allowed into refrigerators or storerooms for the simple fact that the opportunity may prove too tempting and items may disappear. People would love to help themselves to all those steaks in you walk-in before they go on a camping trip, and maybe someone did not get off in time to visit the liquor store before the big party.

Anytime you see an employee in one of these areas with a bag or box of some kind, it is a good idea to make them justify the behavior. Do not be afraid to ask to look in the bag. A search policy should be part of your company policies for these very reasons. (For more information on this consult your human resource department or your attorney.) If they say no, you have very good reason to be alarmed. At that point, follow the advice and training of your HR department or attorney to make sure the situation is resolved in a professional and legal manner.

Keeping Valuable Inventory Locked Up

One of the simplest steps you can take to prevent theft is to keep product that is not being used locked up and restrict who has access to this product. This applies to any valuable inventory that a bar carries and includes beer, wine, and liquor, as well as mixers such as energy drinks, to expensive soft drinks.

Space of course can be at a premium in a bar, so you will need to think through where the liquor is to be locked up. One of the best solutions is behind the bar itself. A cabinet below the bar offers ease and speed of access. This means that liquor can be had quickly simply by calling over the manager.

Beyond this, a locking cabinet in a back room is another great place to keep liquor stored. A plastic, metal or even plywood cabinet will work. These are inexpensive, light, and will keep people out and the product safe.

Another great way to lock up extra liquor is with a metro shelf security cage. Metro shelving is easy to assemble, very available and reliable commercial shelving. The advantage of this type of shelving is that it is very customizable. There are modifications that allow shelves on the racks to be enclosed with a door. For more information on this type of option, consult a store fixture dealer's catalog.

Beer and wine can easily be secured by simply adding a lock to the cooler in which it is kept. Almost every walking cooler latch will have a hole for the addition of a padlock. If they yours does not, you can always have a hasp added very easily. This simple, inexpensive security investment can quickly protect much of the inventory that would normally be a powerful temptation to theft.

You need to carefully think about, and decide who will have access to this restricted inventory. Remember, that anyone who has access to these areas will be very able to steal from you. In most cases, this access should only be granted to managers who have proven their reliability and integrity.

It is a good idea to keep any **unneeded** inventory locked up. However, you need to make sure that you are not going overboard and making your bar run less efficiently. For example, if a bartender runs out of well vodka, bartenders will not generally keep the customer waiting. In most cases, they will simply pour the least expensive premium vodka in its place. In a situation like this, the efforts to prevent theft have created waste. To prevent situations like this, always make sure your bar starts each day with enough product, but not too much to create the idea that nothing will be missed.

Daily Inventories

Daily inventories are an absolute must when running a tight ship and controlling your cost ratios. In short order, daily inventories are simply the tracking of specific liquor, beer or wine inventories everyday.

Now, obviously, a full inventory is a process that requires far too much time conduct on a daily basis. Were you to do so, you would lose so much time and productivity to make the whole exercise pointless and maybe costly. What you can do, however, is take inventory of several different products everyday. These can be bottles beers, bottles of wine or liquors. For both ease and accuracy, I would recommend that you focus your efforts on easily measured products. Bottles of wine or beer, as well as liquor bottles, would do nicely. Kegs, by their very nature, do not make measuring the contents very easy.

You can weigh the bottles, or you can also take a quick visual inventory. If your bar has a computerized point of sale system, you can run a report that tells you how much of each liquor was sold the night before. This can then be compared to what you had on hand yesterday and what you have on hand today.

For example, yesterday you had 15 shots of whiskey in a bottle. Today you have 5. However, you computer system only registered five shots were sold. Where are the other five? These could have been wasted, or they could have been stolen. If they aren't in the POS it is one or the other. Either way, your daily inventory has revealed an irregularity that needs to be explained. This is why daily inventories are so important and useful.

Don't always inventory the same bottles month after month. If you only inventory the same three liquors forever, it is very possible you are missing one that is being wasted or stolen. It is a good idea to switch things up every 30 days or so. This will keep things fresh and give you a better total picture.

Also, keep which liquors are being inventoried a secret if you can, but not that daily inventories are happening. A little paranoia will go a long way to keeping your bartenders and servers in line and honest.

Set A Good Example

It is above paramount importance, that you as the manager, and any assistants that you might have set a good example for the staff. It does not even matter if you own the bar. You should always be seen paying for each and everything you consume. Many companies permit mangers to have a free shift meal. Of course, this does not need to be paid for, but everything else does and you need to follow the proper procedure for getting your shift meal.

You can help make a show of this by asking for a receipt. This will show people a real dedication to making sure that everything is above board. It will draw people's attention and hopefully they will take their cues from you.

Knowing What Your Employees Drink

It is a good habit for bar managers to get in, to know what their employees drink when they are not working and when they have just finished their shift. This is important information to have, because these are the liquors that will be stolen for personal consumption.

These liquors are also perfect candidates to be monitored through daily inventories. If your employees know that you are watching the bottles that they like to drink from, you will significantly reduce the chances of your business losing money through theft in this manner.

Anti-Theft Training

When you hire a new employee, their training period is often what sets the tone for their entire employment with your company. You need to make sure that you train them that stealing is not tolerated and there are systems in place to catch them. You need to train them to be scared enough not to try and steal.

This is best handled by having a written policy concerning what is expected of them in the area of cash handling. It seems silly, but you actually need to provide them with a piece of paper that spells out what needs to be paid for and what can be had for free (most restaurants and bars permit employees free drinks such as sodas). Also, you as the manager, when presenting them with this policy, should add that you take matters such as this very seriously and violations of this policy will not be tolerated. Also, refer to the fact that you have systems in place to catch thieves. Don't be too specific, after all you don't want them to know your system well enough to beat it, but make sure they will be a little paranoid. This can often go a long way to reducing potential theft in the long run and making your new employee a long tenured, productive investment.

Quick Bottle Counts

Quick bottle counting, is as the name implies, just counting the physical bottles that you have in your bar. This technique will help make sure that bottles are not being taken home by employees or workmen, and will quickly catch such theft.

The best way to implement this type of plan is to do it twice a day. You or your assistants should count the bottles at opening, and again at closing. You also need to have a system of checks and balances in place. The person who counts at night should not be the same person who counts the next morning. This is not a time consuming process, and will only take a few minutes. If you have workmen in your bar overnight, you should also make a special point of counting the bottles after they have left, and before your employees arrive. This will help determine, if any theft is occurring while they are there as well. Cleaning crews and maintenance people can just as easily steal from you and need to be carefully monitored.

Non-Alcohol Personal Drink Theft

It is very common in the restaurant and bar industry to permit employees to receive free soda, coffee, and tea (hot or iced). The cost of these products is generally so low, that it in no way impacts the bottom line, and when caffeinated, helps keep the staff alert and energetic.

However, there are many types of beverages in a bar (that are not alcoholic) that are very popular with employees that can quickly eat into your cost ratios when stolen. These are energy drinks, milkshakes, juices, and espressos. Energy drinks alone can easily cost $5 a can! All of these drinks are expensive and are very popular after a late night when opening a bar.

It is very important that you as the manager establish that these drinks are not free and must be paid for. How you go about this can be something you discuss with your human resources department or attorney. Then, once you have established that these items must be paid for, treat anyone caught drinking one without a receipt, as anyone else who steals. You will only need to make someone the example and the problem will most likely go away. Once you have this situation under control, simply remain vigilant. It can be tempting to look the other way on a little point like this, but don't. You cannot afford to avoid this issue.

Avoid Tip Pools

Tip pooling can be common in bars without computer systems. A tip pool is simply the practice of all employees combining their tips and then being split equally. Tip pools can be a haven for thieves that should be avoided. There are a few reasons that this is the case.

First, every employee participates in a tip pool. This means that you cannot isolate and examine each server or bartender. This provides cover that a thief can hide behind. If you have to suspect everyone, you are already lost.

The second reason that you want to avoid tip pools is that they can offer a psychological rationale for a thief. By adding stolen money to a tip pool, a thief makes everyone culpable in the theft. This can offer comfort enough to permit someone who would not have stolen to begin stealing.

Lastly, employees often know things you will not. They may know that someone on the staff is already stealing. This means that when the tips are being split, they benefit from theft already. They may not feel comfortable reporting the activities of the thief and so quietly accept the stolen money. Over time, this will also break down their reservations to theft. Before long, all of your staff may feel comfortable stealing. This is a worst case scenario, but is also a real possibility.

Checks & Balances

An absolutely necessary concept when trying to prevent theft is the notion of checks and balances. This is the same concept that banks use to make sure people stay honest. It will work in your bar or restaurant too.

Basically, checks and balances is the notion that the information supplied by one person is independently verified by another. For example, a common example in a bar is counting banks. A manager will give a bank to a bartender and the bartender will count it. When the bank is returned, the manager will count it again. This is a system of checks and balances that ensures the bag of money contains the correct amount.

Continuing the bank example, at the end of the night, the manager counts all the banks and locks them in a safe. In the morning, the morning manager also counts them. This double responsibility system makes sure that everyone is double checking everyone else's work and will catch any problems quickly.

When trying to fight theft, it is good to make sure that there are verifications to any information you get. Inventories should be double counted and reported by different people. Information should be verified. You need to check up on your assistants. Ask one bartender to do a bottle count while at the same time asking another. Compare their counts. Do they match?

Building systems that take advantage of checks and balances will go a long way to keeping people honest.

Manager Supervision

Observation Is The First Line Of Defense

One of the best ways that you can prevent theft is to be very observant. This can be hard in a busy bar. However, even in a busy environment, you can watch what is going on and draw conclusions from your observations.

Many managers spend too much time in the back office. This is a mistake. A good manager will have a very palpable presence on the floor. The servers and bartenders will know that they are being watched. This doesn't need to be an intimidating presence. You can walk around. Talk to guests, help to run food or drinks, bus tables and help with the many other chores of running a busy restaurant. However, while you are doing these things, you can listen to what is going on, and watch your employees.

Remember, just being seen, and being constantly present will dissuade many thieves and keep people on their best behavior. This makes your job that much easier.

Beyond just being a presence on the floor of a restaurant; whenever you suspect someone of stealing, start your investigation by simply observing. Spend a night watching what they do as casually as possible. In many cases, you will see what you suspect very quickly. In other cases, you will be able to exonerate the person. However, observation should always be the first step you take when you have suspicions. Remember that.

Asking Questions Is Your Next Line Of Defense

Going hand in hand with observation is asking questions. I cannot stress enough how important this is to creating an environment that is difficult to steal in. Whenever you see a behavior that you do not understand or that seems suspicious, stop and ask some questions. Do this immediately. This is not something that can wait. If you do, you will often lose the opportunity, or forget about it.

This is really very easy to do, but can take a little practice to get comfortable with. Stop the employee. Tell them what you saw and ask them to explain it. Make sure that you do not sound accusatory. This can put someone needlessly on the defensive. Make sure you use a calm, fair and even tone. Instead, approach the problem from the point of view that you do not understand, and need the employees help to do so. After all, there may be a completely reasonable explanation. Many odd, but completely understandable, occurrences can happen in a busy bar over the years. This is something you should remember.

Tracking Transactions

Restaurant POS system software will also have the ability to track specific transactions. This includes voids, comps, walkouts, cancels, etc. Along with this type of information you can also track specific item sales, no sales and other very useful information. Using this information you can often spot odd and suspicious patterns that can help steer you towards a thief.

For example, say that you run a report that looks at all the voids over a month. All of your employees are listed. However, one of your employees has voided out three times as many things as anyone else and only works half as much. This is a departure from the normal pattern that needs to be explained. There could be an innocent reason for it. Perhaps a large party changed their mind and left. Perhaps they accidentally rang in a large drink order by mistake. Who knows? However, there could be nefarious reasons that explain this as well. It is the job of a responsible, diligent manager to find out and explain why. Also, if the person is simply careless, but not stealing, this is still a good find. You have identified a weak link that you can now help to improve with more training and coaching.

Another good example would be a bartender with many more "no sales" than their coworkers. Maybe people just ask them for change more than anyone else, but again it is your job to find out and make sure all is as it should be.

When going through this kind of information, you need to think like a detective. Ask questions and look for patterns that do not belong. Make it known to your employees that you are looking at this information. Post relevant information on a bulletin board. This will put everyone on notice that you are paying attention and will catch a thief. When thieves think they might get caught, they tend to avoid theft.

Know Your Employees

A good manager knows their staff and likes them. These are not machines that work for you, they are people. You should get to know them. In the long run, personal connections will often help to ensure long term, productive employment. However, knowing your staff is a great way to prevent or catch theft early on.

Substance Abuse

It is sad, but true that many people in this world have substance abuse problems. This is true in the restaurant and bar industry as well. You should be familiar with the signs of drug and alcohol abuse and watch for it in your employees. An employee with a drug habit is bad for morale, a danger to themselves and others, and is a dangerous theft potential. If you see signs of this behavior, follow your company's protocols and deal with the matter quickly. Leaving this problem to fester can cost your bar lots of money and does nothing to help the employee that is using, or the staff as a whole.

Excessive Tipping Out

In the restaurant and bar industry, it is not uncommon to tip your coworkers for helping you make money. Typical examples would be hosts, busboys, bartenders and cooks. Every establishment will have their own culture regarding tipping out and what is an appropriate amount.

However, when an employee is excessively generous with their tip outs, this can be an indication of something else and should be investigated. For example, someone is constantly giving five times the normal tip amount to a busboy. This is uncharacteristic. You should start by observing and then begin asking questions.

Bragging About Tips

When I was a tipped employee, I never liked to advertise how much I made. I just looked at this as a private matter. However, others do not always share this philosophy. Many times at the end of a shift people like to advertise, compare and even brag about the amount of money they made. Normally, this is harmless. However, sometimes someone who has just stolen a bunch of money from the bar will be dumb enough to actually brag about it too. Again, you do not have to be very smart to steal. Keep your ears open and when you do hear about excessive tips being made. Do some observing and ask some questions. Often, it is nothing, but sometimes you will catch a stupid thief.

Make A Show Of Tracking Liquor

Marking Bottles

Marking bottles with a permanent marker is an extremely simple and cheap method to help keep track of liquor in a bar. It also can give you a very good idea of what is happening when you are not around.

One night, go and mark all of your bottles with a marker. If you are testing your employees to see if they are stealing, do this discreetly. The next morning, come back in and run a report on your computer system. See what has been sold and compare that to the bottle levels. Do they match? If not, you have good evidence that something is not right and you should do some more digging.

Another great use for marking bottles is just to make your employees nervous. If you go around marking bottles right in front of them, they will conclude that you are tracking liquor sales. This will make anyone who was thinking about stealing much less likely to do so simply because they will be afraid you will catch them.

Tracking Empty Bottles

Tracking empty bottles is another really good way to track what is being poured in your bar. Additionally, in theory, tracking empty bottles allows you to track each and every bottle in your bar from when it comes in to when it goes out.

A common practice in many bars is for the manager to record when bottles are emptied (often termed "broken"). This is not a bad system to get in place. It is common for managers to have the bartenders store the bottles in a special place and only once they have been recorded can they be recycled. This is a good example of checks and balances.

You can record the empty bottle information in a spreadsheet. Adding dates as to when the bottle was emptied will allow you to compare this information to sales information from a POS system.

If you add a method for the spreadsheet to record purchases of alcohol as well (say when you get an order), you will expand this tracking program to become a running inventory.

Even if you do not record the information or only write down what was emptied and when, on a piece of paper, this practice also makes thieves and potential thieves uncomfortable. They may think twice about stealing if they see that you are paying attention and care about your inventory. For this reason alone, tracking empty bottles is a great idea. It demonstrates to your employees that you are paying attention to the liquor and they may be caught if they choose to begin helping themselves to your bar's products.

Ask Your People To Do Counts

Remember that you only need to make a show of tracking your product to be truly effective at discouraging theft. For example, one day, if you have assistant managers, ask them to do a quick bottle count or maybe do a bottled beer inventory. Tell them that you want them to call, email or write the results down for you. Assume they do it, and you do nothing with the information. Well, do they know that you did nothing with the information, or do they think that you are tracking your inventory? Obviously, they believe that you are tracking. This will help to make them less likely to steal, and if other employees see them doing this, they also will be less comfortable with theft.

You can also have bartenders do counts. Now, since they are the people that are likely to be committing theft, you need to make sure they know their results will be verified, or that you already know the count.

As an example, say you have two bartenders one day. Have one of the bartenders do a morning count of bottled beer. Then, you count the bottled beer in the afternoon and compare the results to a sales report from the POS system. Again, this is check and balance.

Additionally, you could also tell your night bartender that a cleaning crew is coming in I and you want to make sure nothing is stolen. So you are asking them to do a count. Tell them that you will recount everything in the morning.

These are just ideas that you can modify, expand and develop to your particular bar. However, remember, anytime that you can demonstrate or even trick your staff into the belief that you are tracking your inventory and will know if something is missing, it is good for your cost ratios and the profitability of your bar.

Computer Systems

Bar computer systems like this one can help control theft in your bar, while at the same time making your bar more profitable and efficient.

For a bar owner (or manager) there is really no greater investment that you can make than a computerized point of sale system (POS). These systems offer you control in your bar that would have been unimaginable 25 years ago.

A computerized POS system involves a database driven computer program operated on a central server and several computer terminals throughout the bar and restaurant. On these terminals, servers and bartenders enter their orders and the information is transmitted to the bar printers or the kitchen for preparation. These systems are fully customizable and the program can be adapted for fit into any hospitality situation with customer programmable menus, prices, reports etc. These computer systems also act as time clocks for your employees.

Everything in the last paragraph is great and makes running a bar much easier. However, from the point of view of this book, the best part about a POS system is that it becomes a record of every action that is carried out in a bar. This information is then available for use by the manager in the prevention of waste and theft. Additionally, these computer systems throw up additional obstacles to thieves.

Keeping & Tracking Paper Receipts

If your bar does not have a computerized POS system, you will most likely be using paper tickets. This is often the case with small family owned bars and restaurants. This is a low cost system that can be used effectively; you just need to take some precautions.

First, you need to make sure that you have paper tickets that will be appropriate to preventing theft. These tickets should have a unique number on each one. This will help you keep track of them. You also need to make sure your tickets allow the customer to have a receipt while at the same time leaving you with a copy.

There are two types of paper tickets that will fill this requirement. The first of these has a tear of slip of paper at the bottom of the ticket. This portion can be torn off and given to the customer as a receipt. The top portion is then retained by the bar or restaurant. The other type of ticket is a multi-page carbon copy ticket. Each ticket will consist of two or three pages. The third page is useful when you need to pass a copy of the ticket to a kitchen. This kitchen copy can then be thrown away, while still leaving a copy for the house and the server. Make sure your bar uses on of these systems to prevent theft.

Independent Compliance Checks

One of your goals as a manager is to construct realistic, effective systems that prevent theft and control waste. Even the best system in the world is only effective when it is used. The strongest prison in the world becomes useless if the front gate is left unlocked.

You will also find that many employees will follow procedures when you are around and looking, but fail to do so when they are not being watched. A great help to any management teams efforts to enforce these policies is outside, independent and secret monitoring of the service and policy compliance in your bar. This is achieved through the use of a mystery shopping agency.

Mystery shopping is simple. First you hire a firm. Then the firm will send in its agent on a schedule that you decide (monthly, weekly, bi-weekly, etc.) and they will report on what they see. The criteria of the report are dictated by you, the client and can incorporate anything you like.

Great examples of questions to include in a mystery shopping report are:

- What was the name of your server or bartender?

- Were you given a receipt?

- Was a check placed in front of you while you sat at the bar?

- Did the bartender ring in the drink before it was poured?

- Were any charges on the ticket written by hand? (Obviously, this only applies in bars without a POS system)

- Did the bartender measure the drink you were given?

Finding a mystery shopping firm is not difficult. You can consult the phonebook, but more convenient these days is the Internet. By simply using the search engine of your choice and the location of your restaurant of bar, you will be able to find plenty of local mystery shopping companies. Not all mystery shopping firms are the same. To make sure the company you are dealing with is reliable, ask for references. Check these references. Also make sure to shop around for a good price.

Manager Pop-Ins

As a manager, your employees will naturally act differently around you than they do when you are not around. Often, when a manger is not around, people become more relaxed and complacent. This is a situation that can breed both the bad behaviors of theft and waste.

A great tool to combat this inevitable effect is to conduct pop-ins. This is where you, as the manager, make a habit of randomly appearing in your restaurant or bar to check up and make sure everyone is behaving as they should. This creates a feeling that you could show up at any time and things better be running well when you do.

It is not a bad idea to conduct this type of action several times a month. Be careful not to establish a pattern. Remember, we want to foster uncertainty. To do this, we must be random. Most of the time, you will find that your employees are happy to see you, and business is carrying on as it should.

Random Check Audits

It is a great habit for you and your assistant managers to be in the habit of conducting random check audits. This is when you access a check in the POS system and compare what is on the check to what is on the table. If they have salads or appetizers, is it reflected on the check? Are the desserts on the check? What about the sodas?

This is a "look and see" operation that can reveal many problems in your bar not just with theft. Often, servers are in a hurry and can forget. This will help remind them that you are looking and that they need to pay attention to little details like ringing things in. After all, this is money we are talking about.

If you do this over a period of time, you will learn which servers have problems with this. Additionally, if you make it known that you are doing this, many people will give a long second thought to the idea of trying to steal anything this way.

Video Surveillance Systems

Many large businesses such as casinos and hotels are big fans of video surveillance systems. These offer many advantages. In the first place, their very presence is enough to scare many thieves out of the practice. Additionally, they can be used to track inefficiencies in the work habits of your employees and identify problems in the flow of your bar. Lastly, these can be very useful in recording the events in your bar. The bar business can be litigious and having an ironclad record of events that a video surveillance systems offers can be of great help.

Small security camera housings like this one, even it they do not have a camera in them, will scare many people out of theft.

It used to be true that video surveillance systems were very expensive, bulky, and difficult to install. That is not true anymore. Cameras have become amazingly small and inexpensive. Additionally, using wireless technologies, there is little more to do than provide electricity to a camera. The video feed can then be sent wirelessly to a recording station in a secure back room. You can even buy complete video surveillance kits for a few hundred dollars at an electronics store.

Even if you do not want to put cameras in your bar for some reason, there is nothing to say that you cannot place decoy housings. These are simply the empty camera housings like the one on page 101. However, they have no camera in them. This alone is more than enough to scare many people straight.

Confronting An Employee When You Suspect Theft

There is no black and white way that you can confront an employee that you suspect of theft. Confronting an employee in a situation like this can very easily lead to that employees dismissal. You should take this very seriously because the law takes this very seriously. If you act in a manner that is improper, you could face legal complications down the road.

If your company has a human resources department, always make sure that you talk to them. Present your evidence and discuss things before proceeding. First, always follow your company's guidelines. Never go off half cocked and make a blatant accusation or fire someone without checking with HR.

If you are an independent bar owner, you need to be even more cautious. In most cases, you will not have a human resources department that you can speak with. This means that you have less in the way of resource to work with. However, it is likely that you will have an attorney that you have worked with. If this is the case, these people can provide you with excellent information (for a fee of course).

Lastly, you may consider hiring a firm to handle you HR matters. This is never a bad investment in society as in love with lawsuits as ours. These companies will provide you with HR services as needed, on a periodic basis, for a fee. Additionally, many of these firms offer HR compliance contact numbers where you can speak with an HR representative immediately. You will still have to do the confrontation, and possibly the termination, but you will be able to receive competent advice and make sure you are in compliance with all laws before proceeding.

Conclusion

Theft can be one of the most angering occurrences in a bar. Employees that you have hired and would like to be able to trust stealing from your business (whether you own or just manage) can be infuriating. Beyond that, this is criminal activity that can cost your bar big money if you do not prevent it.

In this chapter we have discussed many of the types of theft that can occur, as well as ways to stop it. Beyond that, we have talked about how to make your workplace inhospitable to a thief. Remain vigilant and never let your guard down. As soon as you do, someone will take advantage of it.

Check Out These Other Great Titles From Pratzen Publishing
Available at www.pratzenpublishing.com

Vending Machine Fundamentals: How To Build Your Own Route
by Steven Woodbine

This book is a complete guide to building your own full service vending business based on soda and snack machines. This book walks you through goals, financing, corporate structure, vending business models, maintenance, service vehicles, inventory management, business analysis, and writing a business plan.

__$19.95__

Vending Machine Fundamentals Volume II: Success Strategies For Building Your Own Bulk Route
By Steven Woodbine

This is the second volume in the Vending Machine Fundamentals series. This book explains in simple English how to build and manage your own bulk vending business. This books covers who a bulk vending business is right for, various machine types, product lines, inventory management and the specific particulars of managing a bulk vending route.

__$18.95__

Making Money With Storage Auctions

By Edward Busoni

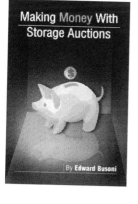

It is not common knowledge that every day across America, hundreds of storage lockers are auctioned off to winning bidders. The property in these units is often sold at tiny fractions of what the goods are actually worth. Inside this book, the author explains how you can start and profit from a storage auction business. Best of all a business of this type can be started for almost nothing!

__$18.95__

Fundamentals Of Offshore Banking: How To Open Accounts Almost Anywhere
By Walter Tyndale

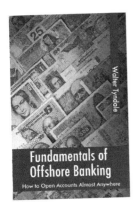

This book explores the global banking industry. Inside the covers you will find information on why you might want to open an account in a foreign country, how to do so, and advice on how to protect your deposit. Additionally, many of the countries that will accept foreign deposits are profiled with information about banking regulators and institutions.

<u>$19.95</u>

How To Live A Debt Free Life: Get Out Of Debt And Stay Out Of Debt
By Peter Wilmore

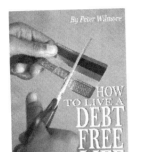

Learn how to free yourself from debt forever inside the pages of this book. The author of this book overcame his own debt and explains how through common sense and careful money management, you can too. In addition, there are chapters about starting to invest for retirement and how to protect yourself and family with insurance.

<u>$19.95</u>

Bartending Basics: A Complete Beginner's Guide
By Thomas Morrell

This book is a how-to guide written by ten year veteran of the restaurant and bar industry. Inside you will learn all about beer, wine and distilled spirits, as well as bartending techniques, ways to remember recipes, responsible bartending, cost and crowd control. There is also a chapter about how to put together a resume and how to find a job to start your new career.

<u>$19.95</u>

Printed in Poland
by Amazon Fulfillment
Poland Sp. z o.o., Wrocław

57540306R00063